Study Guide (Chapters 1-10)

College Accounting

EIGHTEENTH EDITION

James A. Heintz, DBA, CPA

Professor of Accounting, University of Kansas

Lawrence, Kansas

Robert W. Parry, Jr., PhD

Professor of Accounting, Indiana University

Bloomington, Indiana

THOMSON

SOUTH-WESTERN

Australia · Canada · Mexico · Singapore · Spain · United Kingdom · United States

THOMSON

SOUTH-WESTERN

Study Guide with Working Papers for College Accounting, 18th Edition, Chapters 1-10
James A. Heintz and Robert W. Parry

VP/Editorial Director:
Jack W. Calhoun

VP/Editor-in-Chief:
George Werthman

Publisher:
Rob Dewey

Acquisitions Editor:
Jennifer Codner

Sr. Developmental Editor:
Sara Wilson

Sr. Marketing Manager:
Larry Qualls

Sr. Production Editor:
Tim Bailey

Marketing Channel Manager:
Bryan Joyner

Media Technology Editor:
Jim Rice

Media Developmental Editor:
Sally Nieman

Media Production Editor:
Robin Browning

Editorial Assistant:
Janice Hughes

Printer:
Thomson-West

Art Director:
Michelle Kunkler

Manufacturing Coordinator:
Doug Wilke

Cover Designer:
Lisa Albonetti,
Cincinnati, OH

Cover Images:
© PhotoDisc, Inc.

Composition:
Marci Combs

For more information about our products, contact us at:

Thomson Learning Academic Resource Center

1-800-423-0563

Thomson Higher Education
5191 Natorp Boulevard
Mason, OH 45040
USA

Table of Contents

CHAPTER 1
INTRODUCTION TO ACCOUNTING

LEARNING OBJECTIVES

Chapter 1 is designed to introduce you to accounting—its purpose, process, and career opportunities. Businesses that keep good accounting records benefit in many ways. Users of accounting information are able to make sound decisions, which will affect the business's future. Accounting offers many career opportunities, some of which are entry-level and task-oriented and others that involve decision making and planning.

Objective 1.   Describe the purpose of accounting.
   Accounting is the process by which businesses keep track of daily transactions and determine how the business is doing. Accounting provides needed information for its many users, from owners to government agencies and others.

Objective 2.   Describe the accounting process.
   The accounting process contains six major steps:
   Step 1   Analyzing: Looking at information available and figuring out what to do with it. This first step in the accounting process usually occurs when the business receives some type of information, such as a bill, that needs to be properly entered into the business's records. This first step also involves deciding if the piece of information should result in an accounting entry or not.
   Step 2   Recording: Entering the information, manually or via a computer, into the accounting system.
   Step 3   Classifying: Grouping like things together.
   Step 4   Summarizing: Bringing together all information items to determine a result, such as profit or loss.
   Step 5   Reporting: Communicating the results, such as profit or loss, commonly using tables of numbers to tell the financial status of the business.
   Step 6   Interpreting: Examining the financial statements to evaluate the financial health of the business.

Objective 3. Define GAAP and describe the process used to develop these principles.
        Generally accepted accounting principles (GAAP) are the rules that businesses must follow when preparing financial statements. The Securities and Exchange Commission (SEC) has the legal power to make these rules for firms listed on one of the U.S. stock exchanges. However, the SEC has delegated this responsibility to the Financial Accounting Standards Board (FASB).

FASB takes the following steps to develop an accounting standard.
   1.   The issue is placed on FASB's agenda.
   2.   After researching an issue, FASB issues a Discussion Memorandum.
   3.   To gather additional views on the issue, the Board often holds **public hearings** around the country.
   4.   Following these hearings, the Board issues an Exposure Draft. This document explains the rules that FASB believes firms should follow in accounting for this event.
   5.   After considering feedback on the Exposure Draft, the Board issues a final Statement of Financial Accounting Standards (SFAS).

Objective 4.   Define three types of business ownership structures.
   Businesses can be classified according to who owns them and the specific way they are organized. A sole proprietorship is owned by one person who assumes all risks for the business and makes all business decisions. A partnership is owned by two or more persons who share the risks and decision making. Corporations have many owners (shareholders) whose risk is limited to their investment and who have little influence in business decisions.

Objective 5.   Classify different types of businesses by activities.

Businesses also can be classified by the type of service or product they provide. A service business provides a service, a merchandising business purchases a product from another business to sell, and a manufacturing business makes a product to sell.

Objective 6.   Identify career opportunities in accounting.

Accounting has varied and diverse opportunities, depending on the education and experience of the worker, the type of business, and the accounting processes used within the business.

Accounting clerks record, sort, and file accounting information. Bookkeepers supervise clerks, help with daily accounting work, and summarize information. Para-accountants provide many accounting, auditing, or tax services under the direct supervision of an accountant.

Public accountants offer services such as auditing, tax advice, and management consulting. Managerial accountants offer services to private businesses, such as designing accounting information systems, general accounting, cost accounting, budgeting, tax accounting, and internal auditing. Government and not-for-profit organizations also employ accountants.

Accounting is a professional field, which includes organizations and certifications for those who pass examinations and have relevant work experience.

REVIEW QUESTIONS

Instructions: Analyze each of the following items carefully before writing your answer in the column at the right.

Question	Answer

LO 1   1. The purpose of accounting is to provide current information to users. For each user below, briefly describe what type of information is needed.

    a. Owners (present and future)

    b. Managers who make decisions for the business

    c. Creditors (present and future)

    d. Government agencies (state, local, and national)

LO 4   2. A travel agency is an example of this type of business...................... _____

LO 4   3. The ownership structure where owners share risks and decision making is called a(n) _____. .... _____

LO 5   4. A(n) _____ business makes a product to sell.............................. _____

LO 5   5. A business that purchases a product from another business to sell to customers is called a(n) _____ business...................................... _____

LO 4   6. Under the _____ ownership structure, the owner's personal assets can be taken to pay creditors.. _____

LO 3   7. The Financial Accounting Standards Board develops procedures and guidelines called _____ to be followed in the accounting process. _____

LO 5 8. The following actions are taken by the FASB when developing an
accounting standard. Indicate the proper sequence of events by
placing a 1 through 5 in the space provided.

Step

_____ The Statement of Financial Accounting Standards (SFAS) is issued.

_____ **Public hearings** are held.

_____ An **Exposure Draft** is issued.

_____ The issue is placed on FASB's agenda.

_____ A **Discussion Memorandum** is issued.

LO 4 9. The owner's risk is usually limited to their initial investment in this
Type of ownership structure.. _____

LO 6 10. By meeting education and experience requirements, and passing an
examination, a public accountant can achieve recognition as a(n) _____ . _____

LO 2 11. The six major steps of the accounting process are listed in the box at
the right. In front of each term, write the letter that identifies the
correct description provided in the column on the left.

a. The process of entering financial information about events
affecting the business

b. The process of bringing together various items of information
to determine a result

c. The process of sorting or grouping like things together, rather
than merely keeping a simple, diary-like narrative record of
numerous and varied transactions

d. The process of determining the effect of various events on
the business

e. The process of deciding the importance of the information in
various reports

f. The process of communicating the results of operations

_____ Analyzing

_____ Recording

_____ Classifying

_____ Summarizing

_____ Reporting

_____ Interpreting

CHAPTER 2
ANALYZING TRANSACTIONS:
THE ACCOUNTING EQUATION

LEARNING OBJECTIVES

Chapter 2 continues the introductory discussion of accounting—its elements, equation, and transactions. The accounting equation provides a structure for analyzing transactions. After all transactions have been analyzed, the financial statements—income statement, statement of owner's equity, and balance sheet—are prepared. Let's look at each of these learning objectives in detail.

Objective 1.   Define the accounting elements.

Accounting elements are the parts that make up the accounting equation: assets, liabilities, and owner's equity. **Assets** are items *owned* by the business that will provide future benefits. **Liabilities** are debts *owed* by the business and will require a future outflow of assets. **Owner's equity** (also called net worth or capital) is the difference between assets and liabilities. **Revenues** represent the amount a business charges customers for products sold or services provided. Revenues create an inflow of assets. **Expenses** represent an outflow of assets (or increase in liabilities) as a result of the efforts made to generate revenues.

Objective 2.   Construct the accounting equation.

The accounting equation shows the relationship among assets, liabilities, and owner's equity (the accounting elements):

$$\textbf{Assets} = \textbf{Liabilities} + \textbf{Owner's Equity}$$

When given two of the numbers for the equation above, you can calculate the missing number by adding or subtracting.

The accounting equation may be expanded to include revenues, expenses, and drawing. Although drawing is not considered a major element in the accounting equation, it is a very special type of owner's equity account. It represents the withdrawals of assets from the business by the owner.

Assets		=	Liabilities	+	Owner's Equity			
Items Owned			Amounts Owed		Owner's Investment + Earnings			
Cash +	Delivery Equipment	=	Accounts Payable	+	Jessica Jane, Capital	− Jessica Jane, Drawing	+ Revenues	− Expenses

Objective 3.   Analyze business transactions.

Analyzing is the first step in the accounting process. Three questions must be answered: (1) What happened? (2) Which accounts are affected, and what kind of accounts are they (asset, liability, owner's equity)? (3) How is the accounting equation affected? (Accounts will increase or decrease, but the equation always remains in balance.)

Objective 4.   **Show the effects of business transactions on the accounting equation.**

Each transaction will affect asset, liability, owner's equity, revenue, or expense accounts. For example, when an owner invests cash in the business, the asset account called *Cash* increases, and the owner's equity account *Capital* also increases.

For each transaction, you must decide what accounts are affected and whether the accounts increase or decrease. After each transaction, the equation must still be in balance.

Objective 5.   **Prepare and describe the purposes of a simple income statement, statement of owner's equity, and balance sheet.**

After the transactions are completed, the financial statements are prepared to show the results of those transactions. All financial statements have a heading that indicates the name of the firm, title of the statement, and time period or date covered by the statement. The income statement reports revenues, expenses, and the net income for the period. The statement of owner's equity shows the beginning balance of the owner's capital account, plus investments and net income, less withdrawals to compute the ending capital balance. The balance sheet reports all assets, liabilities, and the owner's capital on a certain date and confirms that the accounting equation has remained in balance.

Objective 6.   **Define the three basic phases of the accounting process.**

The three basic phases of the accounting process are input, processing, and output. The inputs to the accounting process are the business transactions. These transactions are processed to recognize their effects on the assets, liabilities, owner's equity, revenues, and expenses of the business. The results of these events are then reported as outputs of the accounting process in the financial statements.

REVIEW QUESTIONS

Instructions: Analyze each of the following items carefully before writing your answer in the column at the right.

	Question	**Answer**
LO 2 1.	The entire accounting process is based on one simple equation called the _____.	_____
LO 1 2.	An individual, association, or organization that engages in business activities is called a(n) _____.	_____
LO 1 3.	An item owned by a business that will provide future benefits. is a(n) _____	_____
LO 1 4.	Something owed to another business entity is a(n) _____.	_____
LO 1 5.	A(n) _____ is an unwritten promise to pay a supplier for assets purchased or a service rendered.	_____
LO 1 6.	The amount by which assets exceed the liabilities of a business	_____
LO 1 7.	According to the _____ concept, nonbusiness assets and liabilities are not included in the business entity's records.	_____
LO 2 8.	Assets – liabilities = _____.	_____
LO 2 9.	Assets – owner's equity = _____.	_____
LO 2 10.	Assets = liabilities + _____.	_____

LO 4 11. The outflow of assets (or increase in liabilities) as the result
of efforts to produce revenue is called a(n) _____. ....   _____

LO 4 12. When total revenues exceed total expenses, the difference
is called..   _____

LO 4 13. When expenses are greater than revenues, the difference is called.   _____

LO 4 14. Any accounting period of twelve months' duration is called a(n)...   _____

LO 4 15. Withdrawals, or _____, represent a reduction in owner's equity
because the owner takes cash or other assets for personal use......   _____

LO 5 16. The financial statement that reports the profitability of the
business for a period of time is the _____. ....   _____

LO 5 17. The financial statement that shows investments and withdrawals by
the owner, as well as profit or loss generated by the business, is the   _____

LO 5 18. The financial statement that reports the assets, liabilities, and
owner's equity on a specific date is the _____. ....   _____

LO 5 19. On the balance sheet, assets are listed in order of _____, or the
ease with which they can be converted to cash. ....   _____

EXERCISES AND PROBLEMS

Exercise 1 (LO 2) THE ACCOUNTING EQUATION

Using the accounting equation provided below, compute the missing amounts.

	ASSETS	=	LIABILITIES	+	OWNER'S EQUITY
(a)	_____	=	$ 4,000	+	$20,000
(b)	$25,000	=	$8,000	+	_____
(c)	$50,000	=	_____	+	$10,000

Exercise 2 (LO 2/4) THE EXPANDED ACCOUNTING EQUATION

Using the accounting equation provided below, compute the missing amounts.

	ASSETS	=	LIABILITIES	+	CAPITAL	–	DRAWING	+	REVENUE	–	EXPENSES
(a)	_____	=	$60,000	+	$20,000	–	$10,000	+	$80,000	–	$60,000
(b)	$80,000	=	_____	+	$35,000	–	$ 5,000	+	$70,000	–	$55,000
(c)	$90,000	=	$25,000	+	_____	–	$ 2,000	+	$57,000	–	$50,000
(d)	$60,000	=	$20,000	+	$30,000	–	$ 5,000	+	_____	–	$40,000
(e)	$40,000	=	$25,000	+	$40,000	–	$ 5,000	+	$30,000	–	_____
(f)	$75,000	=	$20,000	+	$50,000	–	_____	+	$40,000	–	$25,000

Exercise 3 (LO 5) STATEMENT OF OWNER'S EQUITY

If owner's equity was $38,000 at the beginning of the period and $45,000 at the end of the period, compute the net income or loss for the period. (There were no investments or withdrawals during the period.)

Exercise 4 (LO 2) ACCOUNTING EQUATION

If Irma Elkton, a dentist, owns office equipment amounting to $3,500, laboratory equipment amounting to $10,000, and other property that is used in the business amounting to $4,620, and owes business suppliers a total of $5,000, the owner's equity in the business is:

Exercise 5 (LO 2) ACCOUNTING EQUATION

One year later, the amount of Dr. Elkton's business assets has increased to a total of $22,000, and the amount of business liabilities has increased to a total of $6,000. Assuming that Dr. Elkton has not made any additional investments or withdrawals, compute:

(a)   Owner's equity at year end $ _____

(b)   Net income or loss for the year $ _____

Exercise 6 (LO 3/4) EFFECTS OF TRANSACTIONS (BALANCE SHEET ACCOUNTS)

Rich Brite has started his own business. During the first month, the following transactions occurred:

(a)   He invested $15,000 cash in the business, and the money was used
       to open a bank account.
(b)   Purchased office equipment for cash, $4,000.
(c)   Purchased a computer on account for $9,000.
(d)   Paid $2,000 on account for the office equipment.

Using the lines provided below, show the effect of each transaction on the basic elements of the accounting equation: assets, liabilities, and owner's equity. Compute the new amounts for each element after each transaction to satisfy yourself that the accounting equation has remained in balance.

	ASSETS	=	LIABILITIES	+	OWNER'S EQUITY
(a)	_____		_____		_____
Bal.	_____		_____		_____
(b)	_____		_____		_____
Bal.	_____		_____		_____
(c)	_____		_____		_____
Bal.	_____		_____		_____
(d)	_____		_____		_____
Bal.	_____		_____		_____

Exercise 7 (LO 3/4) EFFECTS OF TRANSACTIONS (REVENUE, EXPENSE, WITHDRAWALS)

In late May, Glen Ross opened a business by investing $20,000 cash and purchasing office equipment on account for $8,000. These events were properly entered in the accounting records. In June, the following transactions took place.

(a) Ross received $4,000 from a client for professional services rendered.

(b) Ross paid $1,200 office rent for the month.

(c) Ross paid $200 to the power company for the month's utility bill.

(d) Ross withdrew $600 cash for personal use.

On the first Balance (Bal.) line provided below, record the amount of assets, liabilities, and owner's equity as the result of Ross's investment and purchase of office equipment in May. Then, record the effect of transactions (a) to (d) on the expanded accounting equation: Assets = Liabilities + Owner's Equity [Capital – Drawing + Revenues – Expenses]. Compute the new balances for each category after each transaction to satisfy yourself that the accounting equation has remained in balance.

			OWNER'S EQUITY				
			GLEN ROSS,	GLEN ROSS,			
	ASSETS	= LIABILITIES +	CAPITAL	– DRAWING	+ REVENUES	– EXPENSES	DESCRIPTION
Bal.							
(a)							
Bal.							
(b)							
Bal.							
(c)							
Bal.							
(d)							
Bal.							

Exercise 8 (LO 3/4) EFFECTS OF TRANSACTIONS (ALL ACCOUNTS)

Judith Moore started her own business. During the month of July, the following transactions occurred.

(a) Invested $10,000 cash in the business.

(b) Purchased office equipment for $5,500 on account.

(c) Received $900 cash from a client for services rendered.

(d) Purchased computer equipment for cash, $6,000.

(e) Received $1,500 cash from a client for services rendered.

(f) Paid $800 office rent for the month.

(g) Paid the telephone bill for the month, $75.

(h) Paid $100 on account, for office equipment previously purchased.

(i) Moore withdrew $500 for personal use.

Exercise 8 (Concluded)

Required:

1. Record the effect of each of the transactions from the previous page on the accounting equation provided in the chart below. Compute the new balances for the accounts after each transaction to satisfy yourself that the equation has remained in balance.

	ASSETS		= LIABILITIES +		OWNER'S EQUITY				
	Cash	+ Office Equipment =	Accounts Payable	+ J. Moore, Capital –	J. Moore, Drawing	+ Revenues –	Expenses	Description
(a)								
Bal.								
(b)								
Bal.								
(c)								
Bal.								
(d)								
Bal.								
(e)								
Bal.								
(f)								
Bal.								
(g)								
Bal.								
(h)								
Bal.								
(i)								
Bal.								

2. After recording the above transactions, compute the following:

Total assets...$ _____

Total liabilities..$ _____

Owner's equity...$ _____

Owner's equity in excess of original investment....................$ _____

Total revenues..$ _____

Total expenses..$ _____

Net income...$ _____

Exercise 9 (LO 5) PREPARATION OF AN INCOME STATEMENT

Based on the transactions reported in Exercise 8, prepare an income statement for Judith Moore Enterprises for the month ended July 31, 20—, in the form provided below.

Exercise 10 (LO 5) PREPARATION OF THE STATEMENT OF OWNER'S EQUITY

Based on the transactions reported in Exercise 8, prepare a statement of owner's equity for Judith Moore Enterprises for the month ended July 31, 20—, in the form provided below.

Exercise 11 (LO 5) PREPARATION OF A BALANCE SHEET

Based on the transactions reported in Exercise 8, prepare a balance sheet as of July 31, 20—, in the form provided below.

Problem 12 (LO 2) THE ACCOUNTING EQUATION

Dr. Abe Miller is a general practitioner. As of December 31, Miller owned the following assets related to the professional practice:

Cash	$3,300	X-ray equipment	$7,000
Office equipment	4,500	Laboratory equipment	4,000

As of that date, Miller owed business suppliers as follows:

General Office Equipment Inc.	$2,000
Young Medical Supply Company	1,500
Buck Gas Company	1,200

Required:

1. Compute the amount of assets, liabilities, and owner's equity as of December 31.

   ASSETS   =   LIABILITIES   +   OWNER'S EQUITY

   _____   _____   _____

2. Assuming that during January there is an increase of $4,600 in Dr. Miller's business assets and an increase of $2,500 in business liabilities, compute the resulting accounting equation as of January 31.

   ASSETS   =   LIABILITIES   +   OWNER'S EQUITY

   _____   _____   _____

3. Assuming that during February there is a decrease of $1,500 in assets and a decrease of $1,200 in liabilities, compute the resulting accounting equation as of February 28.

   ASSETS   =   LIABILITIES   +   OWNER'S EQUITY

   _____   _____   _____

4. Assuming that Dr. Miller made no additional investments or withdrawals, compute the net income or loss for each month.

Problem 13 (LO 3/4) EFFECT OF TRANSACTIONS ON ACCOUNTING EQUATION

Susan Cole started her own consulting business in October, 20—. During the first month, the following transactions occurred.

(a) Invested $12,000 cash in the business.
(b) Purchased office equipment for $7,500 on account.
(c) Purchased computer equipment for cash, $800.
d) Received $700 cash from a client for services rendered.
(e) Paid $600 office rent for the month.
(f) Paid student assistant wages for the month, $150.
(g) Paid one year insurance premium, $200.
(h) Paid $3,000 on account for the office equipment purchased in (b).
(i) Cole withdrew cash for personal use, $100.

Problem 13 (Concluded)

Required:

1. Record the effect of each of the transactions from the previous page on the accounting equation chart provided below. Compute the new amounts in the accounts after each transaction to satisfy yourself that the equation has remained in balance.

	Cash	+	Office Equip.	+	Prepaid Insur.	=	Accounts Payable	+	S. Cole, Capital	–	S. Cole, Drawing	+	Revenues	–	Expenses	Description
	ASSETS					= LIABILITIES +			OWNER'S EQUITY							
(a)																
Bal.																
(b)																
Bal.																
(c)																
Bal.																
(d)																
Bal.																
(e)																
Bal.																
(f)																
Bal.																
(g)																
Bal.																
(h)																
Bal.																
(i)																
Bal.																

2. After recording the transactions, compute the following.

Total assets..$ _____

Total liabilities..$ _____

Owner's equity...$ _____

Change in owner's equity from original investment...................$ _____

Total revenues..$ _____

Total expenses..$ _____

Net income (loss)..$ _____

Problem 14 (LO 5) INCOME STATEMENT

Based on the transactions in Problem 13, prepare an income statement for Susan Cole Consulting Services for the month ended October 31, 20—, in the form provided below.

Problem 15 (LO 5) STATEMENT OF OWNER'S EQUITY

Based on the transactions in Problem 13, prepare a Statement of Owner's Equity for Susan Cole Consulting Services for the month ended October 31, 20—, in the form provided below.

Problem 16 (LO 5) BALANCE SHEET

Based on the transactions in Problem 13, prepare a balance sheet as of October 31, 20—, in the form provided below.

Problem 17 (LO 3/4/5) ANALYZE THE EFFECTS OF BUSINESS TRANSACTIONS ON THE ACCOUNTING EQUATION AND PREPARE FINANCIAL STATEMENTS

Stuart Cassady is opening a typing service. During the first month (April, 20—), the following transactions occurred.

(a) Stuart invested $10,000 in the business.

(b) Purchased office supplies for $200 cash.

(c) Purchased office supplies for $800, $400 on account and $400 in cash.

(d) Received typing fees of $300 cash.

(e) Paid the rent, $600.

(f) Withdrew $100 for personal use.

(g) Earned typing fees of $600, $200 in cash and $400 on account.

(h) Made partial payment for office supplies in (c) of $200.

(i) Received $200 cash for typing fees earned on account in (g).

Required:

1. Record the effect of each transaction on the accounting equation below. Compute new amounts in accounts after each transaction.

	ASSETS			= LIABILITIES +		OWNER'S EQUITY				
	Cash +	Accounts Receivable +	Office Supplies =	Accounts Payable +	S. Cassady, Capital −	S. Cassady, Drawing +	Revenues −	Expenses	Description
(a)									
Bal.									
(b)									
Bal.									
(c)									
Bal.									
(d)									
Bal.									
(e)									
Bal.									
(f)									
Bal.									
(g)									
Bal.									
(h)									
Bal.									
(i)									
Bal.									

Problem 17 (Concluded)

2. Based on the transactions in part 1 of Problem 17, prepare an income statement, statement of owner's equity, and balance sheet for Stuart Cassady.

CHAPTER 3
THE DOUBLE-ENTRY FRAMEWORK

LEARNING OBJECTIVES

Objective 1.   Define the parts of a T account.

The **T account** gets its name from the fact that it resembles the letter *T*. There are three major parts of an account. The title of the account is on top. The left side of the T account is the debit side, and the right side is the credit side.

Objective 2.   Foot and balance a T account.

To determine the balance of a T account, simply total the dollar amounts of the debit and credit sides. These totals are known as **footings.** The difference between the footings is called the *balance* of the account. The balance is written on the side with the larger footing.

Objective 3.   Describe the effects of debits and credits on specific types of accounts.

Assets are on the left side of the accounting equation. Thus, increases are entered on the left, or debit, side; and decreases are entered on the right, or credit, side. The normal balance of an asset account is a debit.

Liabilities and owner's equity are on the right side of the equation. Thus, increases are entered on the right, or credit, side; and decreases are entered on the left, or debit, side. The normal balance of a liability and owner's equity account is a credit.

Revenues increase owner's equity. Thus, increases in revenue are recorded as credits. The normal balance of a revenue account is a credit.

Expenses decrease owner's equity. Thus, increases in expenses are recorded as debits. The normal balance of an expense account is a debit.

Withdrawals of cash and other assets by the owner for personal reasons decrease owner's equity. Thus, an increase in drawing is recorded as a debit. The normal balance of a drawing account is a debit.

The following figure should be helpful in developing your understanding of debits and credits and the accounting equation.

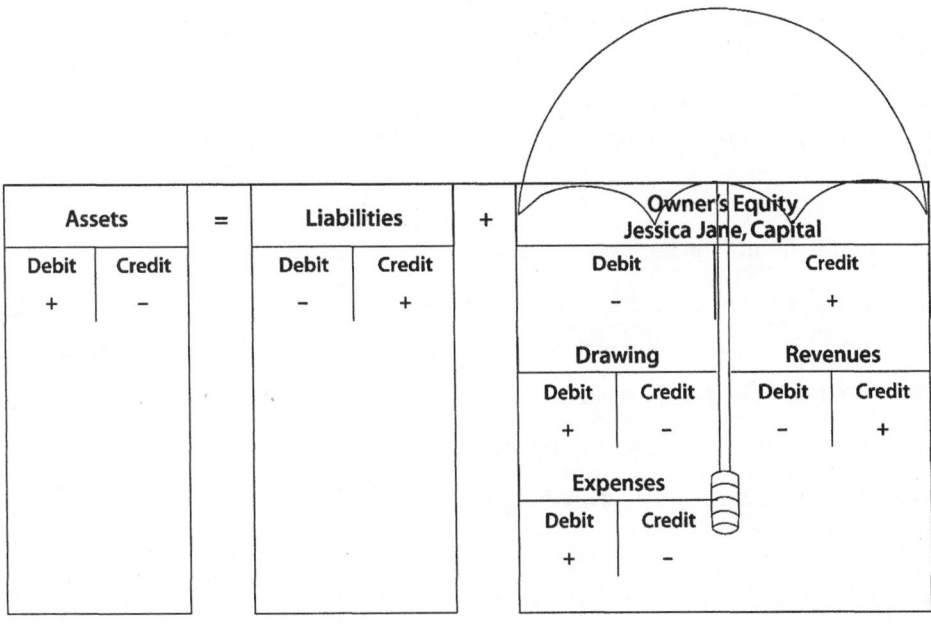

Objective 4.   Use T accounts to analyze transactions.

There are three basic questions that must be answered when analyzing a transaction: (1) What happened? (2) Which accounts are affected? and (3) How is the accounting equation affected? After analyzing the transaction, in every instance, debits will equal credits.

Objective 5.   Prepare a trial balance and explain its purposes and linkages with the financial statements.

There are two very important rules in double-entry accounting: (1) The sum of the debits must equal the sum of the credits. This means that at least two accounts are affected by each transaction. (2) The accounting equation must remain in balance.

A **trial balance** is a list of all accounts showing the title and balance of each account. The total debits and credits must be equal. A trial balance is not a formal statement or report. It can be used as an aid in preparing the financial statements.

REVIEW QUESTIONS

Instructions: Analyze each of the following items carefully before writing your answer in the column at the right.

	Question	**Answer**
LO 4 1.	The fact that each transaction has a dual effect on the accounting elements provides the basis for what is called _____.	_____
LO 1 2.	A form or record used to keep track of the increases and decreases in each type of asset, liability, owner's equity, revenue, and expense is known as a(n) _____.	_____
LO 1 3.	The left side of a T account is called the _____ side.	_____
LO 1 4.	The right side of a T account is called the _____ side.	_____
LO 2 5.	The process of entering totals in the debit and credit side of a T account is referred to as _____.	_____
LO 2 6.	The amount of the difference between the debits and credits recorded in a T account is called the _____.	_____
LO 3 7.	An increase in the asset cash is recorded by a(n) _____.	_____
LO 3 8.	An increase in the liability accounts payable is recorded by a(n).......	_____
LO 5 9.	A list of all of the accounts showing the title and balance of each account is called the _____.	_____
LO 3 10.	The normal balance of a revenue account is on the _____ side. ...	_____
LO 3 11.	A decrease in the liability accounts payable is recorded by a(n)........	_____
LO 3 12.	The normal balance of a liability account is on the _____ side. ...	_____

EXERCISES AND PROBLEMS

Exercise 1 (LO 3) EFFECTS OF DEBITS AND CREDIT

Indicate whether each of the following types of accounts would normally have a debit or credit balance by circling either debit or credit in the column at the right:

Type of Account	Normal Balance (Circle one)	
(a) Assets..	Debit	Credit
(b) Liabilities...	Debit	Credit
(c) Owner's Equity..	Debit	Credit
(d) Revenues..	Debit	Credit
(e) Expenses..	Debit	Credit

Exercise 2 (LO 1) DEFINING THE PARTS OF THE T ACCOUNT

Provided below are T accounts for the five types of accounts discussed to this point. Identify the debit and credit side of each type of account by writing debit on the debit side and credit on the credit side.

Assets	Liabilities	Owner's Equity	Expenses	Revenues

Exercise 3 (LO 3) INCREASING AND DECREASING ACCOUNTS WITH DEBITS AND CREDITS

Provided below are T accounts representing the five types of accounts discussed. Indicate how each account would be increased and decreased by placing a (+) or (–) on the debit and credit side of each account.

Assets	Liabilities	Owner's Equity	Expenses	Revenues

Exercise 4 (LO 4) USING T ACCOUNTS TO ANALYZE TRANSACTIONS

The following transactions were completed by Jacque Hamon, an educational consultant. Analyze each transaction and enter the amounts in the proper debit and credit positions in the T accounts at the right.

(a) Hamon invested $3,000 cash in the business.

Cash	Jacque Hamon, Capital

(b) Received $1,000 in cash for consulting services rendered.

Cash	Professional Fees

(c) Bought office equipment from Gusse Supply Co. on account, $500.

Office Equipment	Accounts Payable

(d) Paid electric bill, $75.

Cash	Utilities Expense

Exercise 4 (Continued)

(e)   Paid Gusse Supply $200 on account.

Cash		Accounts Payable	

(f)   Received $300 in cash for consulting services
rendered.

Cash		Professional Fees	

(g)   Borrowed $1,000 from bank by signing a note.

Cash		Notes Payable	

(h)   Paid the telephone bill, $50.

Cash		Telephone Expense	

Exercise 5 (LO 4) USING T ACCOUNTS TO ANALYZE TRANSACTIONS (BALANCE SHEET ACCOUNTS)

Connie Sung has started her own typing business. During the first month, the following transactions occurred.

(a)   Connie invested $12,000 cash in the business, and the money was deposited in a bank account.
(b)   A new computer and printer were purchased on account from Stahl Electronics for $8,000.
(c)   Paid the premium on a one year insurance policy on computer equipment, $75 cash.
(d)   A bank loan was secured by signing a note for $5,000.
(e)   A $3,000 payment was made to Stahl Electronics on account.

Required:

Record the above transactions in the T accounts provided below.

Assets		=	Liabilities		+	Owner's Equity	
Debit	Credit		Debit	Credit		Debit	Credit
+	−		−	+		−	+

Cash		Accounts Payable		C. Sung, Capital	

Office Equipment		Notes Payable	

Prepaid Insurance	

Exercise 6 (LO 4) USING T ACCOUNTS TO ANALYZE TRANSACTIONS (ALL ACCOUNTS)

In late April, Frazier Baar opened a psychiatry practice by investing $9,000 cash and purchasing a couch, chair, and leather covered note pad on account for $2,500. These events were properly entered in the accounting records. In May, Dr. Baar began seeing patients and entered into the following transactions.

(a) Received $500 for counseling services rendered.
(b) Paid $100 for *Psychology Today* and other magazines for patients to read in the waiting room.
(c) Paid $1,200 office rent for the month.

Required:

1. Enter the balances as of May 1 in the following accounts: Cash, Office Furnishings, Accounts Payable, and F. Baar, Capital.

2. Record the May transactions in the accounts listed below.

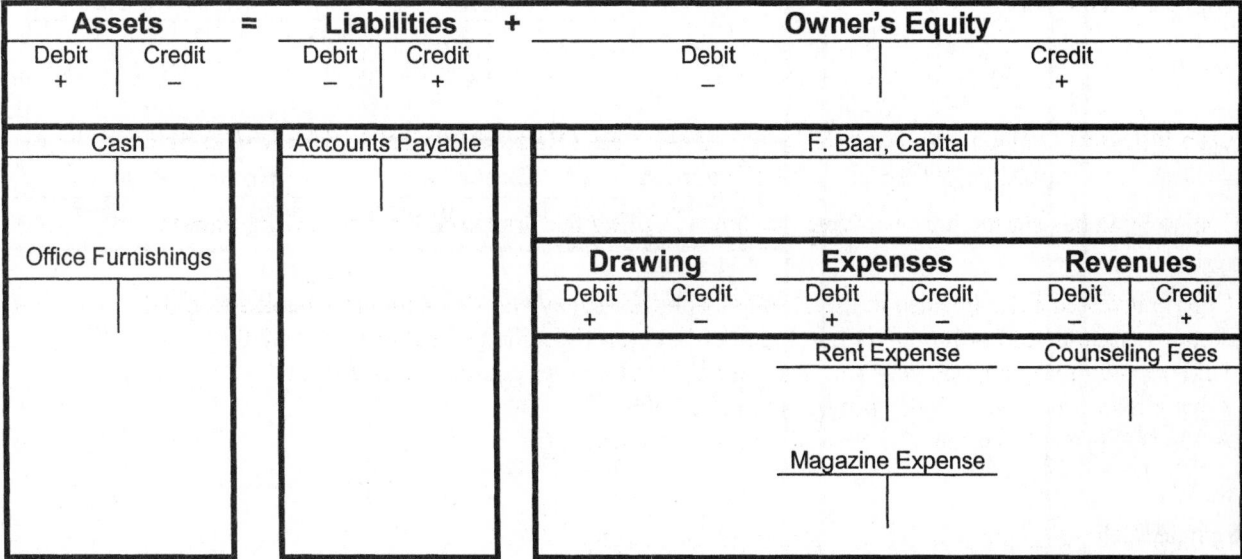

Exercise 7 (LO 2/4) USING T ACCOUNTS TO ANALYZE TRANSACTIONS, FOOTING AND BALANCING T ACCOUNTS.

In January, 20—, Blanca Estavez, CPA, started her own accounting practice. The following is a list of transactions for the first month.

(a) Invested $20,000 cash in the business.
(b) Purchased office supplies, $500 cash.
(c) Purchased office furniture, $6,000 cash.
(d) Purchased a computer and printer for $9,000: $5,000 cash and $4,000 on account.
(e) Paid $800 for accounting software programs.
(f) Performed accounting services and earned fees totaling $1,800: $1,200 in cash and $600 on account.
(g) Paid $700 rent for the month.
(h) Withdrew $200 for personal use.
(i) Paid $2,000 on account for the computer.

Exercise 7 (Continued)

Required:

1. Record the transactions in the T accounts that follow.
2. After all transactions have been entered, foot and balance the T accounts.

Assets	=	**Liabilities**	+	**Owner's Equity**	
Debit +	Credit −	Debit −	Credit +	Debit −	Credit +

Cash	Accounts Payable	B. Estavez, Capital

Accounts Receivable		**Drawing**		**Expenses**		**Revenues**	
		Debit +	Credit −	Debit +	Credit −	Debit −	Credit +

	B. Estavez, Drawing	Rent Expense	Accounting Fees

Office Supplies

Office Furniture

Computer Equipment

Computer Software

Exercise 8 (LO 5) PREPARE A TRIAL BALANCE

Based on the transactions recorded in Exercise 7, prepare a trial balance at the end of the first month of operations using the form provided below.

ACCOUNT	DEBIT BALANCE	CREDIT BALANCE

Problem 9 (LO 2/4/5) ANALYZING TRANSACTIONS WITH T ACCOUNTS, FOOTING AND BALANCING ACCOUNTS, AND PREPARING A TRIAL BALANCE

Jali Abdul has decided to offer his services as a promoter for local rock-n-roll bands. Following is a narrative of selected transactions completed during January, the first month of J.A. Productions' operations.

(a) Abdul invested $10,000 in the business and opened a checking account.

(b) Office furniture was purchased on account at a cost of $5,000.

(c) Computer equipment was purchased for $4,500. Abdul paid $1,500 cash and promised to pay the balance over the next three months.

(d) Office supplies were purchased for cash, $350.

(e) Letters were sent to numerous performing groups throughout the region explaining the services available through J.A. Productions. Postage of $200 was paid in cash.

(f) After securing contracts with several groups, Abdul began arranging performances throughout the region. The telephone bill came to $300 and was paid in cash.

(g) Abdul earned promotion revenue of $2,500: $2,000 in cash and $500 on account.

(h) Paid part-time receptionist $600.

(i) Withdrew $1,000 for personal use.

(j) Abdul paid $2,500 on account for the office furniture.

(k) Collected $250 for promotional fees earned on account.

Required:

1. Record the transactions in the T accounts provided.

2. Foot and balance the accounts.

3. Prepare a trial balance of the accounts as of January 31, 20—, using the form provided.

Problem 9 (Continued)

Assets	=	Liabilities	+	Owner's Equity	
Debit +	Credit −	Debit −	Credit +	Debit −	Credit +

Cash

Accounts Payable

J. Abdul, Capital

Accounts Receivable

Drawing		Expenses		Revenues	
Debit +	Credit −	Debit +	Credit −	Debit −	Credit +

Office Supplies

J. Abdul, Drawing   Wages Expense   Promotion Fees

Office Furniture

Telephone Expense

Computer Equipment

Postage Expense

Problem 9 (Concluded)

ACCOUNT	DEBIT BALANCE	CREDIT BALANCE

Problem 10 REVIEW: ACCOUNTING EQUATION AND FINANCIAL STATEMENTS

Based on the transactions recorded in Problem 9, select the information needed to fill in the blank space in the following statements.

(a)   Total revenue for the month $ _____

(b)   Total expenses for the month $ _____

(c)   Net income for the month $ _____

(d)   Abdul's original investment in the business $ _____

       + the net income for the month $ _____

        – owner's drawing   _____

         increase in capital
                                                     _____

       = owner's equity at the end of the month $ _____

(e)   End-of-month accounting equation:

ASSETS	=	LIABILITIES	+	OWNER'S EQUITY
$_____		$_____		$_____

Problem 11 REVIEW: PREPARATION OF FINANCIAL STATEMENTS

Refer to the trial balance in Problem 9 and to the analysis of the change in owner's equity in Problem 10.

(a)   Prepare an income statement for J.A. Productions for the month ended January 31, 20—.

(b)   Prepare a statement of owner's equity for J.A. Productions for the month ended January 31, 20—.

(c)   Prepare a balance sheet for J.A. Productions as of January 31, 20—.

Problem 11 (Concluded)

CHAPTER 4
JOURNALIZING AND POSTING TRANSACTIONS

LEARNING OBJECTIVES

Chapter 3 introduced the double-entry framework and illustrated the impact of debits and credits on the accounting equation and T accounts. In Chapter 4, business transactions are entered into the general journal and posted to general ledger accounts.

Objective 1. Describe the flow of data from source documents through the trial balance.

The flow of financial data from the source documents through the accounting information systems follows the steps listed below.

1. Analyze what happened by using information from source documents and the firm's chart of accounts.
2. Enter business transactions in the general journal.
3. Post entries to accounts in the general ledger.
4. Prepare a trial balance.

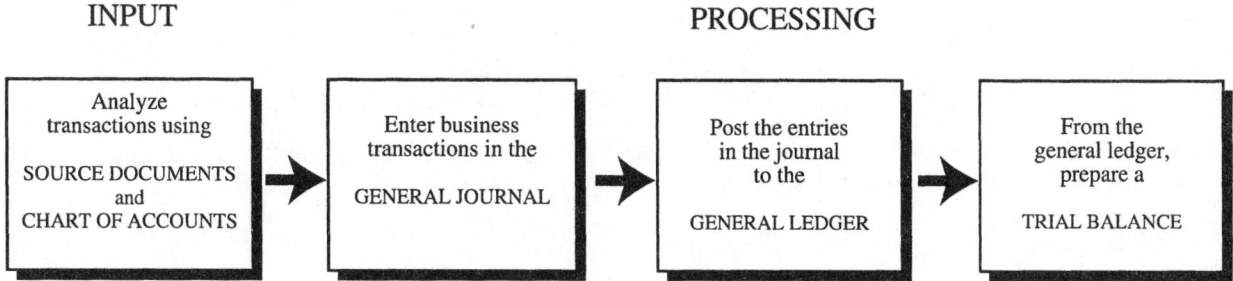

Objective 2. Describe the chart of accounts as a means of classifying financial information.

The **chart of accounts** lists in numerical order all of the accounts being used by a business. Assets are listed first (begin with "1"); liabilities are second (begin with "2"); owner's equity accounts are third (begin with "3"); revenues are fourth (begin with "4"); and expenses are last (begin with "5"). In a three-digit account numbering system, for example, Cash may be account number 101 and Accounts Receivable may be account number 122. Spacing numbers this way permits easy addition of new accounts as the business grows.

Objective 3. Describe and explain the purpose of source documents.

A **source document** provides objective information needed to record a transaction. Examples include check stubs, receipts, cash register tapes, sales invoices, and memos. Source documents are analyzed to determine which accounts should be increased or decreased.

Objective 4. Journalize transactions.

Journalizing is the process of entering information into the journal, or book of original entry. This simply means the journal is the first place a transaction is recorded. The general journal has space to enter the date of the transaction, the name of the accounts being debited and credited, the account numbers, and the amounts of the debits and credits. A brief description follows each journal entry stating the reason for the entry.

Objective 5.   Post to the general ledger and prepare a trial balance.

Once the transactions are entered into the general journal, they must be **posted** to (copied to) the individual accounts, which are located in the general ledger. The accounts are in the general ledger in the chart of accounts order. That is, the assets are first, followed by liabilities, owner's equity, revenue, and expense accounts.

In this chapter, the general ledger accounts are in the form of four-column accounts. This is better than the T account because a running balance is maintained.

The **trial balance** is a listing of account balances at the end of the month—after all the transactions have been posted from the general journal to the general ledger accounts. The total of the debit balances must equal the total of the credit balances.

Objective 6.   Explain how to find and correct errors.

Finding errors can be a long and frustrating process. But there are some methods to reduce the time and effort needed. The first thing to do is double-check your calculations and the accuracy of the posting activities. Common errors include sliding ($230 could become $23 or $2300), and transposing numbers (326 could become 236). Taking the difference between the debits and credits and dividing by 9 or by 2 may help locate the error.

There are two methods of correcting errors. The **ruling method** may be used before the transaction has been posted. Under this method, you draw a line through the incorrect title or amount and write in the correct information above the ruling. The **correcting entry method** is used after an entry has been posted to the general ledger. The correcting entry increases and decreases accounts in a manner that corrects the errors made in previous transactions.

REVIEW QUESTIONS

Instructions: Analyze each of the following items carefully before writing your answer in the column at the right.

Question	Answer
LO 2 1. A list of all the accounts used by a business enterprise is called a(n)...	_____
LO 2 2. Accounts that begin with the number "3" are _____.	_____
LO 2 3. Expenses are accounts that begin with which number?	_____
LO 1 4. A document that provides information about a business transaction is called a(n) _____.	_____
LO 4 5. A document that provides a day-by-day listing of transactions of a business is called a(n) _____.	_____
LO 4 6. A journal is commonly referred to as a(n) _____ because it is here that the first formal accounting record is made.	_____
LO 4 7. Transactions affecting more than two accounts are called _____....	_____
LO 4 8. The act of entering transactions into a journal is called _____....	_____
LO 4 9. In a journal, debits are entered first; then credits are entered and indented _____ (how much space)..............................	_____
LO 5 10. A complete set of all accounts used by a business is known as the	_____
LO 5 11. A(n) _____ account allows the accountant to keep a running balance.	_____

LO 5 12. The process of copying debits and credits from the journal to the ledger accounts is called _____. ....   _____

LO 5 13. Posting from the journal to the ledger is done _____ or at frequent intervals. ....   _____

LO 5 14. The information in the Posting Reference columns of the journal and the ledger accounts provides a link known as a(n) _____.   _____

LO 5 15. A(n) _____ is taken after transactions are posted to the general ledger accounts to be sure that debit and credit balances in the ledger are equal. ....   _____

LO 6 16. A(n) _____ error occurs when you move a number a decimal place to the right or left. ....   _____

LO 6 17. A(n) _____ error occurs when you use the right numbers but in the wrong order. ....   _____

LO 6 18. Drawing a line through the incorrect amount or account title and writing correct information above it is an example of the _____ method. ....   _____

LO 6 19. When an incorrect entry has been journalized and posted, a(n) _____ entry is required. ....   _____

EXERCISES AND PROBLEMS

Exercise 1 (LO 4) REVIEW: TRANSACTION ANALYSIS

Before a transaction is recorded in the journal, it should be analyzed to determine:

(a)   What accounts are affected by the transaction.
(b)   Whether each affected account is to be increased or decreased.
(c)   Whether the increase or decrease is to be accomplished by a debit or credit.

In the following list of transactions for Abbott Service Co., indicate the names of the accounts to be debited and credited. Place a check mark in either the plus (+) or minus (−) column to indicate whether the account has been increased or decreased. The first transaction is entered as an illustration.

Transaction		Account	(+)	(−)
1. J.A. Abbott invested cash in a business enterprise.	Debit:	Cash	√	
	Credit:	J.A. Abbott, Capital	√	
2. Received cash for services provided.	Debit:			
	Credit:			

Transaction		Account	(+)	(−)
3. Paid cash for rent on the office.	Debit:	_____	_____	_____
	Credit:	_____	_____	_____
4. Purchased office equipment on account.	Debit:	_____	_____	_____
	Credit	_____	_____	_____
5. Paid cash to a creditor for a debt previously owed.	Debit:	_____	_____	_____
	Credit:	_____	_____	_____
6. Paid the telephone bill for the month.	Debit:	_____	_____	_____
	Credit:	_____	_____	_____
7. Paid supplier for office equipment purchased in transaction 4 above.	Debit:	_____	_____	_____
	Credit:	_____	_____	_____
8. Paid cash for a car for the owner's personal use.	Debit:	_____	_____	_____
	Credit:	_____	_____	_____
9. Paid temporary secretary's wages.	Debit:	_____	_____	_____
	Credit:	_____	_____	_____
10. Performed services that will be paid for later.	Debit:	_____	_____	_____
	Credit:	_____	_____	_____

Exercise 2 (LO 4) JOURNALIZING TRANSACTIONS

Susan Poe started a business, Poe's Connections. She provides resource referral services whereby she helps businesses locate vendors of specialty products and vice versa. She charges a referral fee to her clients who may be businesses or vendors. She has a part-time clerk who enters information into a database to match requests with potential users or suppliers. Her chart of accounts is as follows:

Assets
  101 Cash
  122 Accounts Receivable
  182 Office Furniture
Liabilities
  202 Accounts Payable

Owner's Equity
  311 Susan Poe, Capital
  312 Susan Poe, Drawing

Revenues
  401 Referral Fees
Expenses
  511 Wages Expense
  521 Rent Expense

Exercise 2 (Continued)

Required:

Enter the following transactions in the two-column journal provided on the next page.

20--

May	1	Susan invested $5,000 cash to start the business.
	5	Purchased office furniture on account, $3,000.
	9	Paid office rent for the month, $450.
	10	Received fees for referral services, $500.
	15	Made payment on account (for office furniture), $100.
	20	Earned referral fees: $125 cash and $175 on account.
	25	Paid wages to clerk for part-time work, $400.
	28	Withdrew cash for personal use, $100.
	29	Received cash for referral services previously rendered, $150.

Exercise 2 (Continued)

GENERAL JOURNAL

PAGE

	DATE		DESCRIPTION	POST. REF.	DEBIT	CREDIT	
1							1
2							2
3							3
4							4
5							5
6							6
7							7
8							8
9							9
10							10
11							11
12							12
13							13
14							14
15							15
16							16
17							17
18							18
19							19
20							20
21							21
22							22
23							23
24							24
25							25
26							26
27							27
28							28
29							29
30							30
31							31
32							32
33							33
34							34
35							35
36							36
37							37

Exercise 3 (LO 5) POST TO THE GENERAL LEDGER

Post the transactions from Exercise 2 to the general ledger accounts provided as follows. Be sure to enter the appropriate cross-reference information in the Posting Reference columns of the general ledger accounts and the general journal.

GENERAL LEDGER

ACCOUNT: Cash   ACCOUNT NO.   101

DATE	ITEM	POST. REF.	DEBIT	CREDIT	BALANCE DEBIT	CREDIT

ACCOUNT: Accounts Receivable   ACCOUNT NO.   122

DATE	ITEM	POST. REF.	DEBIT	CREDIT	BALANCE DEBIT	CREDIT

ACCOUNT: Office Furniture   ACCOUNT NO.   182

DATE	ITEM	POST. REF.	DEBIT	CREDIT	BALANCE DEBIT	CREDIT

ACCOUNT: Accounts Payable   ACCOUNT NO.   202

DATE	ITEM	POST. REF.	DEBIT	CREDIT	BALANCE DEBIT	CREDIT

Exercise 3 (Continued)

GENERAL LEDGER

ACCOUNT: Susan Poe, Capital   ACCOUNT NO.   311

DATE	ITEM	POST. REF.	DEBIT	CREDIT	BALANCE	
					DEBIT	CREDIT

ACCOUNT: Susan Poe, Drawing   ACCOUNT NO.   312

DATE	ITEM	POST. REF.	DEBIT	CREDIT	BALANCE	
					DEBIT	CREDIT

ACCOUNT: Referral Fees   ACCOUNT NO.   401

DATE	ITEM	POST. REF.	DEBIT	CREDIT	BALANCE	
					DEBIT	CREDIT

ACCOUNT: Wages Expense   ACCOUNT NO.   511

DATE	ITEM	POST. REF.	DEBIT	CREDIT	BALANCE	
					DEBIT	CREDIT

ACCOUNT: Rent Expense   ACCOUNT NO.   521

DATE	ITEM	POST. REF.	DEBIT	CREDIT	BALANCE	
					DEBIT	CREDIT

Exercise 4 REVIEW: PREPARE A TRIAL BALANCE

After the transactions are posted in Exercise 3, prepare the trial balance.

ACCOUNT	ACCT. NO.	DEBIT BALANCE	CREDIT BALANCE

Problem 5 (LO 4/5) JOURNALIZING AND POSTING TRANSACTIONS FOLLOWED BY PREPARATION OF A TRIAL BALANCE

Della Jordan started her own business, D.J. Parties. For about $50 per hour, Della and a group of part-time associates serve as disc jockeys for parties held at the client's home. As part of the service, Della provides a lighting system, stereo equipment, compact discs, and two disc jockeys working as a team for each party. A wide range of music is offered, and the client may provide additional tapes or discs to be played. A chart of accounts is provided below.

D. J. Parties
Chart of Accounts

Assets			Owner's Equity		
101	Cash		311	Della Jordan, Capital	
122	Accounts Receivable		312	Della Jordan, Drawing	
181	Stereo Equipment		Revenue		
182	Office Furniture		401	Disc Jockey Fees	
183	Discs and Tapes				
184	Lighting Equipment		Expenses		
185	Van		511	Wages Expense	
			521	Rent Expense	
Liabilities			525	Telephone Expense	
202	Accounts Payable		538	Gas Expense	

Problem 5 (Continued)

The following transactions occurred during May, the first month of operation.

May	1	Jordan invested $30,000 cash in the business. The funds were deposited in a business checking account.
	3	Purchased stereo equipment and speaker systems from Big Al's Discount Stereo for $7,000: $3,000 cash and $4,000 on account.
	4	Purchased compact discs and tapes for $2,500.
	4	Purchased lighting equipment for $2,000.
	5	Purchased office furniture on account, $500.
	7	Purchased a van to be used to haul the equipment to the clients' homes, $9,500.
	18	Earned fees for services rendered, $3,800: $800 cash and $3,000 on account.
	20	Paid part-time associates for work performed, $600.
	21	Made payment on account for stereo equipment bought on May 3, $1,500.
	25	Paid for gas for the van, $40.
	27	Paid telephone bill, $80.
	28	Received cash for services previously rendered, $1,500.
	29	Paid part-time associates $1,100.
	30	Paid rent, $500.
	30	Made payment on account for stereo equipment bought on May 3, $1,200.
	30	Jordan made withdrawal for personal use, $1,000.

Required:

1. Enter the transactions in the two-column journal provided on pages 43–44. Use Journal page 1 for transactions through May 20. Enter the remainder on page 2.

2. Post the transactions from the journal to the four-column ledger accounts on pages 45–48.

3. Prepare a trial balance.

Problem 5 (Continued)

[Instructor: Account numbers in Post Ref. column are entered when completing requirement 2.]

GENERAL JOURNAL

PAGE   1

	DATE		DESCRIPTION	POST. REF.	DEBIT	CREDIT	
1							1
2							2
3							3
4							4
5							5
6							6
7							7
8							8
9							9
10							10
11							11
12							12
13							13
14							14
15							15
16							16
17							17
18							18
19							19
20							20
21							21
22							22
23							23
24							24
25							25
26							26
27							27
28							28
29							29
30							30
31							31
32							32
33							33

Problem 5 (Continued)

GENERAL JOURNAL

PAGE 2

	DATE		DESCRIPTION	POST. REF.	DEBIT	CREDIT	
1							1
2							2
3							3
4							4
5							5
6							6
7							7
8							8
9							9
10							10
11							11
12							12
13							13
14							14
15							15
16							16
17							17
18							18
19							19
20							20
21							21
22							22
23							23
24							24
25							25
26							26
27							27
28							28
29							29
30							30
31							31
32							32
33							33

Problem 5 (Continued)

GENERAL LEDGER

ACCOUNT: Cash   ACCOUNT NO. 101

DATE	ITEM	POST. REF.	DEBIT	CREDIT	BALANCE	
					DEBIT	CREDIT

ACCOUNT: Accounts Receivable   ACCOUNT NO. 122

DATE	ITEM	POST. REF.	DEBIT	CREDIT	BALANCE	
					DEBIT	CREDIT

ACCOUNT: Stereo Equipment   ACCOUNT NO. 181

DATE	ITEM	POST. REF.	DEBIT	CREDIT	BALANCE	
					DEBIT	CREDIT

Problem 5 (Continued)

ACCOUNT: Office Furniture   ACCOUNT NO.   182

DATE		ITEM	POST. REF.	DEBIT	CREDIT	BALANCE	
						DEBIT	CREDIT

ACCOUNT: Discs and Tapes   ACCOUNT NO.   183

DATE		ITEM	POST. REF.	DEBIT	CREDIT	BALANCE	
						DEBIT	CREDIT

ACCOUNT: Lighting Equipment   ACCOUNT NO.   184

DATE		ITEM	POST. REF.	DEBIT	CREDIT	BALANCE	
						DEBIT	CREDIT

ACCOUNT: Van   ACCOUNT NO.   185

DATE		ITEM	POST. REF.	DEBIT	CREDIT	BALANCE	
						DEBIT	CREDIT

ACCOUNT: Accounts Payable   ACCOUNT NO.   202

DATE		ITEM	POST. REF.	DEBIT	CREDIT	BALANCE	
						DEBIT	CREDIT

Name _____

Problem 5 (Continued)

ACCOUNT: Della Jordan, Capital   ACCOUNT NO. 311

DATE	ITEM	POST. REF.	DEBIT	CREDIT	BALANCE DEBIT	CREDIT

ACCOUNT: Della Jordan, Drawing   ACCOUNT NO. 312

DATE	ITEM	POST. REF.	DEBIT	CREDIT	BALANCE DEBIT	CREDIT

ACCOUNT: Disc Jockey Fees   ACCOUNT NO. 401

DATE	ITEM	POST. REF.	DEBIT	CREDIT	BALANCE DEBIT	CREDIT

ACCOUNT: Wages Expense   ACCOUNT NO. 511

DATE	ITEM	POST. REF.	DEBIT	CREDIT	BALANCE DEBIT	CREDIT

ACCOUNT: Rent Expense   ACCOUNT NO. 521

DATE	ITEM	POST. REF.	DEBIT	CREDIT	BALANCE DEBIT	CREDIT

Problem 5 (Concluded)

ACCOUNT: Telephone Expense   ACCOUNT NO. 525

DATE		ITEM	POST. REF.	DEBIT	CREDIT	BALANCE	
						DEBIT	CREDIT

ACCOUNT: Gas Expense   ACCOUNT NO. 538

DATE		ITEM	POST. REF.	DEBIT	CREDIT	BALANCE	
						DEBIT	CREDIT

ACCOUNT	ACCT. NO.	DEBIT BALANCE	CREDIT BALANCE

Problem 6 REVIEW: PREPARATION OF FINANCIAL STATEMENTS

From the information in Problem 5, prepare an income statement, a statement of owner's equity, and a balance sheet.

Problem 6 (Concluded)

Problem 7

1. (LO 6) CORRECTION OF ERRORS: The Ruling Method

The following journal entries were made but not posted. On January 1, $500 cash was withdrawn by the owner for personal use (R.J. Hammond) but was charged to Wages Expense. On January 2, $230 was paid on account. Make corrections using the ruling method.

GENERAL JOURNAL   PAGE

	DATE		DESCRIPTION	POST. REF.	DEBIT	CREDIT	
1	20— Jan.	1	Wages Expense		5 0 0 00		1
2			Cash			5 0 0 00	2
3			Paid R. J. Hammond				3
4							4
5		2	Accounts Payable		3 2 0 00		5
6			Cash			3 2 0 00	6
7			Payment on account				7
8							8

Problem 7 (Concluded)

2. (LO 6) CORRECTION OF ERRORS: The Correcting Entry Method

On January 10, Office Equipment was debited for $800 when the debit should have been to Office Supplies. Since the entry has been posted, show the appropriate correcting entry made in the general journal on January 15.

GENERAL JOURNAL   PAGE

	DATE	DESCRIPTION	POST. REF.	DEBIT	CREDIT
1					
2					
3					
4					
5					
6					
7					
8					

CHAPTER 5
ADJUSTING ENTRIES AND THE WORK SHEET

LEARNING OBJECTIVES

We are coming to the end of the accounting cycle, and certain things must be done at the end of the period that are not done during the regular accounting period. In Chapter 5, adjusting entries and the work sheet are presented.

Objective 1.   Prepare end-of-period adjustments.

In Chapters 2 through 4, we learned how to account for business transactions—events based primarily on arms length exchanges with other parties. During the accounting period, however, other changes occur which affect the financial condition of the business. For example, supplies are being used, equipment is wearing out, insurance is expiring, and employees may have earned wages that have not yet been paid. It is important for information reported on the financial statements to accurately reflect the results of business transactions with outside parties <u>and</u> other activities taking place inside the business. Therefore, adjustments must be made at the end of the accounting period to properly report assets and liabilities on the balance sheet and to comply with the matching principle. This principle requires the matching of revenues earned with expenses incurred to produce the revenues.

Objective 2.   Prepare a work sheet.

The work sheet is a tool used by accountants to help organize work done at the end of the accounting period. This document is not a formal part of the accounting system. Therefore, information recorded here has no affect on the accounts or financial statements. The main purposes of the work sheet are to prepare the adjusting entries and accumulate information that will be used in the preparation of the financial statements. There are five steps taken to prepare a work sheet.

Step 1   Prepare a trial balance to ensure that the general ledger is in balance before adjusting the accounts.

Step 2   Analyze and enter the adjusting entries in the Adjustment columns of the work sheet. Every adjustment must have an equal debit and credit; and on completion, the total debits and credits must be equal in the Adjustment columns.

Step 3   Prepare the adjusted trial balance. Every account appearing in the Trial Balance columns will be extended to the Adjusted Trial Balance columns and include any changes due to the adjusting entries. On completion, the total of the debits and credits in the Adjusted Trial Balance columns must be equal.

Step 4   Extend the balances in the adjusted trial balance to either the Income Statement or Balance Sheet columns. All revenue and expenses are extended to the Income Statement columns. All other accounts (assets, liabilities, owner's capital, owner's drawing) are extended to the Balance Sheet columns.

Step 5   Complete the work sheet. Initially, the totals of the Income Statement columns will not be equal. Similarly, the totals of the Balance Sheet columns will not be equal. If the Income Statement Credit column exceeds the Income Statement Debit column, the difference represents net income. If the Income Statement Debit column exceeds the Income Statement Credit column, the difference represents net loss. The difference in the Balance Sheet columns will be exactly the same as the difference in the Income Statement columns. The amount of net income should be added to the Income Statement Debit column and the Balance Sheet Credit column for total debits to equal total credits for all four columns. If there is a net loss, this amount should be added to the Income Statement Credit column and the Balance Sheet Debit column.

Partial Work Sheet

	For Net Income					For Net Loss			
	Income Statement		Balance Sheet			Income Statement		Balance Sheet	
	Debit	Credit	Debit	Credit		Debit	Credit	Debit	Credit
	2,500	3,200	6,200	5,500		3,000	2,500	7,000	7,500
Net Income	700			700	Net Loss		500	500	
	3,200	3,200	6,200	6,200		3,000	3,000	7,500	7,500

Apart   Together

Objective 3. Describe methods for finding errors on the work sheet.

The following tips may help in finding errors on the work sheet:

1. Check the addition of all columns.
2. Check the addition and subtraction required when extending to the Adjusted Trial Balance columns.
3. Make sure the adjusted account balances have been extended to the appropriate columns.
4. Make sure that the net income or net loss has been added to the appropriate columns.

Objective 4. Journalize adjusting entries.

Once the adjustments have been "penciled in" on the work sheet, the next step is to journalize the adjusting entries. "Adjusting Entries" is written in the Description column in the journal, and the adjusting entries are copied from the work sheet into the journal.

Objective 5. Post adjusting entries to a general ledger.

After the adjusting entries are journalized, the next step is to post them to the general ledger. The word "Adjusting" is written in the Item column in the general ledger, and each adjustment is posted to the proper general ledger account.

REVIEW QUESTIONS

Instructions: Analyze each of the following items carefully before writing your answer in the column at the right.

Question	Answer
LO 1 1. The matching principle in accounting requires the matching of _____ and _____.	_____
LO 1 2. The asset account Supplies is adjusted to the income statement account entitled _____.	_____
LO 1 3. The asset account Prepaid Insurance is adjusted to the income statement account entitled _____.	_____
LO 1 4. The adjustment to Wages Expense will also affect a liability account called _____.	_____
LO 1 5. The period of time a plant asset is expected to help produce revenues is called its _____.	_____
LO 1 6. The purpose of _____ is to spread the cost of a plant asset over its useful life.	_____
LO 1 7. A plant asset's original cost less salvage value is called _____.	_____

LO 1 8. A _____ has a credit balance and is deducted from the related asset account on the balance sheet. .... _____

LO 1 9. The depreciation adjusting entry consists of a debit to Depreciation Expense and a credit to _____. .... _____

LO 1 10. The difference between the original cost of a plant asset and its accumulated depreciation is called _____. .... _____

LO 2 11. A _____ is helpful in preparing end-of-period adjustments and financial statements. .... _____

LO 2 12. The first two monetary columns of a work sheet are called the _____ columns. .... _____

LO 2 13. To which columns of the work sheet are asset and liability accounts extended? .... _____

LO 2 14. To which columns of the work sheet are revenue and expense accounts extended? .... _____

LO 2 15. To which columns of the work sheet are the capital and drawing accounts extended? .... _____

LO 2 16. If the total of the Income Statement Credit column exceeds the total of the Debit column, the business has earned _____. ..... _____

EXERCISES AND PROBLEMS

Exercise 1 (LO 1) PREPARING END-OF-PERIOD ADJUSTMENTS: SUPPLIES

The beginning balance of the supplies account was $300. During the year, additional supplies costing $600 were purchased and entered as debits to the supplies account. An end-of-period inventory determined that $200 worth of supplies are still on hand.

Required:

1. Determine the balance of the supplies account just prior to making any end-of-period adjustments. _____

2. When preparing the balance sheet, what should be reported for Supplies at the end of the year? _____

3. Determine the balance of the supplies expense account just prior to making any end-of-period adjustments. _____

4. When preparing the income statement, what should be reported for Supplies Expense? (What was the cost of the supplies used?) _____

5. What adjustment must be made to the supplies and supplies expense accounts? _____

Exercise 2 (LO 1) PREPARING END-OF-PERIOD ADJUSTMENTS: DEPRECIATION

Office equipment with an expected life of ten years and no salvage value was purchased on January 1 for $5,000. Assume the business has no other office equipment and straight-line depreciation is used.

Required:

1. What is the balance of the office equipment account at the end of the year? _____

2. What expense amount should be reported on the income statement for the use of the office equipment? _____

3. What book value should be reported on the balance sheet for the office equipment at the end of the first year? _____

4. What adjustment must be made at the end of the year to report information about the office equipment on the income statement and balance sheet? _____

Exercise 3 (LO 1/4/5) PREPARING, JOURNALIZING, AND POSTING ADJUSTING ENTRIES: SUPPLIES

The Maddie Hays modeling agency began the current period with office supplies that cost $1,225. During the period, additional supplies costing $4,545 were purchased. At the end of the accounting period, December 31, 20—, only $800 in supplies remain.

Required:

1. Enter the appropriate adjusting entry in a two-column journal.
2. Post this entry to the ledger accounts provided below and on the next page.

GENERAL JOURNAL

PAGE 5

	DATE	DESCRIPTION	POST. REF.	DEBIT	CREDIT	
1						1
2						2
3						3
4						4

GENERAL LEDGER

ACCOUNT: Supplies   ACCOUNT NO. 141

DATE		ITEM	POST. REF.	DEBIT	CREDIT	BALANCE DEBIT	BALANCE CREDIT
20— Jan.	1	Balance	✔			1 2 2 5 00	
Feb.	12		J2	4 5 4 5 00		5 7 7 0 00	

Exercise 3 (Concluded)

ACCOUNT: Supplies Expense   ACCOUNT NO. 524

DATE	ITEM	POST. REF.	DEBIT	CREDIT	BALANCE DEBIT	BALANCE CREDIT

Exercise 4 (LO 1/4/5) PREPARING, JOURNALIZING, AND POSTING ADJUSTING ENTRIES: DEPRECIATION

The Billy Willis Detective Agency began the accounting period by purchasing three cars that cost a total of $75,000. The estimated useful lives of these cars is only two years with no salvage value.

Required:

1. Enter the appropriate adjusting entry at the end of the first year in a two-column journal. Willis uses straight-line depreciation.
2. Post this entry to the ledger accounts provided below.

GENERAL JOURNAL   PAGE 8

	DATE	DESCRIPTION	POST. REF.	DEBIT	CREDIT	
1						1
2						2
3						3
4						4

GENERAL LEDGER

ACCOUNT: Automobiles   ACCOUNT NO. 185

DATE	ITEM	POST. REF.	DEBIT	CREDIT	BALANCE DEBIT	BALANCE CREDIT
20— Jan. 2		J1	75 0 0 0 00		75 0 0 0 00	

ACCOUNT: Accumulated Depreciation—Automobiles   ACCOUNT NO. 185.1

DATE	ITEM	POST. REF.	DEBIT	CREDIT	BALANCE DEBIT	BALANCE CREDIT

Exercise 4 (Concluded)

ACCOUNT: Depreciation Expense—Automobiles   ACCOUNT NO. 541

DATE	ITEM	POST. REF.	DEBIT	CREDIT	BALANCE	
					DEBIT	CREDIT

Exercise 5 (LO 1/4/5) PREPARING, JOURNALIZING, AND POSTING ADJUSTING ENTRIES: PREPAID INSURANCE AND WAGES PAYABLE

On June 1, the Straw Basket Herb Farm purchased a one-year liability insurance policy for $600.

As of June 30, an additional $120 was earned by the employees but not yet paid.

Required:

1. Enter the appropriate adjusting entries at the end of June in the following general journal.

2. Post the entries to the ledger accounts provided.

GENERAL JOURNAL   PAGE 6

	DATE	DESCRIPTION	POST. REF.	DEBIT	CREDIT	
1						1
2						2
3						3
4						4
5						5
6						6
7						7
8						8

Exercise 5 (Concluded)

GENERAL LEDGER

ACCOUNT: Prepaid Insurance   ACCOUNT NO. 145

DATE		ITEM	POST. REF.	DEBIT	CREDIT	BALANCE DEBIT	BALANCE CREDIT
20— June	1		J2	6 0 0 00		6 0 0 00	

ACCOUNT: Wages Payable   ACCOUNT NO. 219

DATE	ITEM	POST. REF.	DEBIT	CREDIT	BALANCE DEBIT	BALANCE CREDIT

ACCOUNT: Wages Expense   ACCOUNT NO. 511

DATE		ITEM	POST. REF.	DEBIT	CREDIT	BALANCE DEBIT	BALANCE CREDIT
20— June	14		J5	5 0 0 00		5 0 0 00	
	28		J5	5 0 0 00		1 0 0 0 00	

ACCOUNT: Insurance Expense   ACCOUNT NO. 535

DATE	ITEM	POST. REF.	DEBIT	CREDIT	BALANCE DEBIT	BALANCE CREDIT

Problem 6 (LO1/2) PREPARING ADJUSTMENTS AND THE WORK SHEET

Kim Ho offers employment counseling to middle managers unemployed due to corporation downsizing. On January 1 of the current year, Ho purchased office equipment with an expected life of 12 years and no salvage value. Computer equipment with an expected life of four years and no salvage value was purchased on July 1 of the current year. Ho uses straight-line depreciation. Office supplies on hand at year-end amounted to $150. Employees earned $300 in wages that have not yet been paid. Provided are the general ledger accounts as of December 31, prior to adjustment.

Required:

1. Using the ledger accounts, complete the Trial Balance columns of the year-end work sheet provided.

2. Prepare the necessary year-end adjustments.

3. Complete the work sheet.

GENERAL LEDGER

ACCOUNT: **Cash**   ACCOUNT NO.   101

DATE		ITEM	POST. REF.	DEBIT	CREDIT	BALANCE DEBIT	BALANCE CREDIT
20— Dec.	1	Balance	✔			2 4 0 0 00	
	21		J20	10 8 0 0 00		13 2 0 0 00	
	27		J20		4 2 0 0 00	9 0 0 0 00	

ACCOUNT: **Office Supplies**   ACCOUNT NO.   142

DATE		ITEM	POST. REF.	DEBIT	CREDIT	BALANCE DEBIT	BALANCE CREDIT
20— Dec.	1	Balance	✔			2 0 0 00	
	6		J20	3 0 0 00		5 0 0 00	

ACCOUNT: **Office Equipment**   ACCOUNT NO.   181

DATE		ITEM	POST. REF.	DEBIT	CREDIT	BALANCE DEBIT	BALANCE CREDIT
20— Dec.	1	Balance	✔			6 0 0 0 00	

ACCOUNT: Accumulated Depreciation—Office Equipment   ACCOUNT NO.   181

DATE	ITEM	POST. REF.	DEBIT	CREDIT	BALANCE DEBIT	BALANCE CREDIT

Problem 6 (Continued)

ACCOUNT: Computer Equipment   ACCOUNT NO. 187

DATE		ITEM	POST. REF.	DEBIT	CREDIT	BALANCE DEBIT	BALANCE CREDIT
20—							
Dec.	1	Balance	✔			8 0 0 0 00	

ACCOUNT: Accumulated Depreciation—Computer Equipment   ACCOUNT NO. 187.1

DATE	ITEM	POST. REF.	DEBIT	CREDIT	BALANCE DEBIT	BALANCE CREDIT

ACCOUNT: Accounts Payable   ACCOUNT NO. 202

DATE		ITEM	POST. REF.	DEBIT	CREDIT	BALANCE DEBIT	BALANCE CREDIT
20—							
Dec.	1	Balance	✔				3 0 0 00
	6		J20		2 0 0 00		5 0 0 00
	27		J20	1 0 0 00			4 0 0 00

ACCOUNT: Wages Payable   ACCOUNT NO. 219

DATE	ITEM	POST. REF.	DEBIT	CREDIT	BALANCE DEBIT	BALANCE CREDIT

ACCOUNT: Kim Ho, Capital   ACCOUNT NO. 311

DATE		ITEM	POST. REF.	DEBIT	CREDIT	BALANCE DEBIT	BALANCE CREDIT
20—							
Dec.	1	Balance	✔				10 2 0 0 00

Problem 6 (Continued)

ACCOUNT: Kim Ho, Drawing   ACCOUNT NO. 312

DATE		ITEM	POST. REF.	DEBIT	CREDIT	BALANCE DEBIT	BALANCE CREDIT
20— Dec.	1	Balance	✔			1 5 0 0 00	
	30		J20	1 0 0 0 00		2 5 0 0 00	

GENERAL LEDGER

ACCOUNT: Counseling Fees   ACCOUNT NO. 401

DATE		ITEM	POST. REF.	DEBIT	CREDIT	BALANCE DEBIT	BALANCE CREDIT
20— Dec.	1	Balance	✔				22 0 0 0 00
	31		J20		10 1 7 0 00		32 1 7 0 00

ACCOUNT: Wages Expense   ACCOUNT NO. 511

DATE		ITEM	POST. REF.	DEBIT	CREDIT	BALANCE DEBIT	BALANCE CREDIT
20— Dec.	1	Balance	✔			7 0 0 0 00	
	31		J20	1 5 0 0 00		8 5 0 0 00	

ACCOUNT: Rent Expense   ACCOUNT NO. 521

DATE		ITEM	POST. REF.	DEBIT	CREDIT	BALANCE DEBIT	BALANCE CREDIT
20— Dec.	1	Balance	✔			4 4 0 0 00	
	4		J20	1 2 0 0 00		5 6 0 0 00	

ACCOUNT: Supplies Expense   ACCOUNT NO. 524

DATE		ITEM	POST. REF.	DEBIT	CREDIT	BALANCE DEBIT	BALANCE CREDIT

Problem 6 (Continued)

ACCOUNT: Utilities Expense   ACCOUNT NO. 533

DATE		ITEM	POST. REF.	DEBIT	CREDIT	BALANCE	
						DEBIT	CREDIT
20— Dec.	1	Balance	✔			1 3 0 0 00	
	31		J20	5 7 0 00		1 8 7 0 00	

GENERAL LEDGER

ACCOUNT: Depreciation Expense—Office Equipment   ACCOUNT NO. 541

DATE	ITEM	POST. REF.	DEBIT	CREDIT	BALANCE	
					DEBIT	CREDIT

ACCOUNT: Depreciation Expense—Computer Expense   ACCOUNT NO. 542

DATE	ITEM	POST. REF.	DEBIT	CREDIT	BALANCE	
					DEBIT	CREDIT

ACCOUNT: Miscellaneous Expense   ACCOUNT NO. 549

DATE		ITEM	POST. REF.	DEBIT	CREDIT	BALANCE	
						DEBIT	CREDIT
20— Dec.	1	Balance	✔			6 0 0 00	
	22		J20	2 0 0 00		8 0 0 00	

Problem 6 (Continued)

KIM HO EMPLOYMENT

WORK

FOR YEAR ENDED

ACCOUNT TITLE	TRIAL BALANCE		ADJUSTMENTS	
	DEBIT	CREDIT	DEBIT	CREDIT
1				
2				
3				
4				
5				
6				
7				
8				
9				
10				
11				
12				
13				
14				
15				
16				
17				
18				
19				
20				
21				
22				
23				
24				
25				
26				
27				
28				
29				
30				
31				

Problem 6 (Continued)
COUNSELING SERVICES

SHEET

DECEMBER 31, 20--

ADJUSTED TRIAL BALANCE		INCOME STATEMENT		BALANCE SHEET		
DEBIT	CREDIT	DEBIT	CREDIT	DEBIT	CREDIT	
						1
						2
						3
						4
						5
						6
						7
						8
						9
						10
						11
						12
						13
						14
						15
						16
						17
						18
						19
						20
						21
						22
						23
						24
						25
						26
						27
						28
						29
						30
						31

Problem 7 (LO 1/2) PREPARING ADJUSTMENTS AND THE WORK SHEET

The trial balance for Juan's Speedy Delivery Service as of September 30, 20— is shown on the work sheet that follows.

Data to complete the adjustments are as follows:

(a)   Supplies inventory as of September 30, $450.
(b)   Insurance expired, $200.
(c)   Depreciation on delivery equipment, $350.
(d)   Wages earned by employees but not paid as of September 30, $215.

Required:

1.   Enter the adjustments in the Adjustments columns on the work sheet.
2.   Complete the work sheet.

JUAN'S SPEEDY

WORK

FOR MONTH ENDED

	ACCOUNT TITLE	TRIAL BALANCE		ADJUSTMENTS	
		DEBIT	CREDIT	DEBIT	CREDIT
1	Cash	1 5 4 5 00			
2	Accounts Receivable	8 5 0 00			
3	Supplies	7 2 5 00			
4	Prepaid Insurance	1 5 0 0 00			
5	Delivery Equipment	6 3 0 0 00			
6	Accum. Depr.—Delivery Equip.				
7	Accounts Payable		9 8 0 00		
8	Wages Payable				
9	Juan Garcia, Capital		9 0 0 0 00		
10	Juan Garcia, Drawing	1 2 0 0 00			
11	Delivery Fees		5 2 4 0 00		
12	Wages Expense	1 4 7 5 00			
13	Advertising Expense	4 2 0 00			
14	Rent Expense	7 5 0 00			
15	Supplies Expense				
16	Telephone Expense	1 8 0 00			
17	Insurance Expense				
18	Repair Expense	1 9 0 00			
19	Oil & Gas Expense	8 5 00			
20	Depreciation Expense—Del. Equip.				
		15 2 2 0 00	15 2 2 0 00		

Problem 7 (Concluded)

DELIVERY SERVICE

SHEET

SEPTEMBER 30, 20--

	ADJUSTED TRIAL BALANCE		INCOME STATEMENT		BALANCE SHEET		
	DEBIT	CREDIT	DEBIT	CREDIT	DEBIT	CREDIT	
							1
							2
							3
							4
							5
							6
							7
							8
							9
							10
							11
							12
							13
							14
							15
							16
							17
							18
							19
							20
							21
							22
							23

Problem 8 (LO 3) FINDING AND CORRECTING ERRORS ON A WORK SHEET

A work sheet for George Green's Landscaping Service follows. It should include these adjustments:

(a)   Ending inventory of supplies as of July 31, $350.
(b)   Insurance expired as of July 31, $225.
(c)   Depreciation on tractor, $460.
(d)   Wages earned but not paid as of July 31, $320.

Required:

Errors have been intentionally placed in this work sheet. Review the work sheet for addition mistakes, transpositions, and other errors and make all necessary corrections

(Note: Errors are intentional.)

GREEN'S LANDSCAPING

WORK

FOR MONTH ENDED

	ACCOUNT TITLE	BALANCE		ADJUSTMENTS	
		DEBIT	CREDIT	DEBIT	CREDIT
1	Cash	1 8 2 5 00			
2	Accounts Receivable	7 2 0 00			
3	Supplies	6 0 0 00			(a) 3 5 0 00
4	Prepaid Insurance	8 5 0 00			(b) 2 2 5 00
5	Tractor	6 5 5 0 00			(c) 4 6 0 00
6	Accum. Depr.—Tractor				
7	Accounts Payable		5 2 0 00		
8	Wages Payable				(d) 3 2 0 00
9	George Green, Capital		8 2 5 0 00		
10	George Green, Drawing	1 2 0 0 00			
11	Landscaping Fees		6 1 0 0 00		
12	Wages Expense	1 5 4 0 00		(d) 3 2 0 00	
13	Advertising Expense	2 5 0 00			
14	Rent Expense	7 7 5 00			
15	Supplies Expense			(a) 3 5 0 00	
16	Telephone Expense	1 4 0 00			
17	Utilities Expense	2 2 0 00			
18	Insurance Expense			(b) 2 2 5 00	
19	Depr. Expense—Tractor			(c) 4 6 0 00	
20	Miscellaneous Expense	2 0 0 00			
21		14 8 7 0 00	14 8 7 0 00	1 3 5 5 00	1 3 5 5 00
22	Net Income				
23					

Problem 8 (Concluded)

SERVICE

SHEET

JULY 31, 20--

	ADJUSTED TRIAL BALANCE		INCOME STATEMENT		BALANCE SHEET		
	DEBIT	CREDIT	DEBIT	CREDIT	DEBIT	CREDIT	
1	1 8 2 5 00				1 8 2 5 00		1
2	7 2 0 00				7 2 0 00		2
3	2 5 0 00				2 5 0 00		3
4	6 5 0 00				6 5 0 00		4
5	6 0 9 0 00				6 0 9 0 00		5
6							6
7		5 2 0 00				5 2 0 00	7
8		3 2 0 00		3 2 0 00			8
9		8 2 5 0 00				8 2 5 0 00	9
10	1 2 0 0 00		1 2 0 0 00				10
11		6 1 0 0 00		6 1 0 0 00			11
12	1 5 4 0 00		1 5 4 0 00			1 8 4 0 00	12
13	2 5 0 00		2 5 0 00				13
14	7 7 5 00		7 7 5 00				14
15	3 5 0 00		3 5 0 00				15
16	1 4 0 00		1 4 0 00				16
17	2 2 0 00		2 2 0 00				17
18	2 2 5 00		2 2 5 00				18
19	4 6 0 00		4 6 0 00				19
20	2 0 0 00		2 0 0 00				20
21	13 3 5 5 00	15 1 9 0 00	2 4 1 7 00	6 4 2 0 00	8 3 4 7 00	8 7 7 0 00	21
22			1 7 2 0 00			1 7 2 0 00	22
23			4 1 3 7 00	6 4 2 0 00	8 3 4 7 00	10 4 9 0 00	23

CHAPTER 5 APPENDIX
DEPRECIATION METHODS

APPENDIX LEARNING OBJECTIVES

In Chapter 5, the straight-line method of depreciation was illustrated. In the appendix to Chapter 5, three additional methods are explained. These methods are used when a different schedule of expenses provides a more appropriate matching with the revenues generated.

Objective 1. **Prepare a depreciation schedule using the straight-line method.**

Objective 2. **Prepare a depreciation schedule using the sum-of-the-years'-digits method.**

Objective 3. **Prepare a depreciation schedule using the double-declining-balance method.**

Objective 4. **Prepare a depreciation schedule for tax purposes using the Modified Accelerated Cost Recovery System.**

Apx. Exercise 1 (LO 1) STRAIGHT-LINE DEPRECIATION

Office equipment was purchased on January 1 at a cost of $48,000. It has an estimated useful life of 4 years and a salvage value of $6,000. Prepare a depreciation schedule showing the depreciation expense, accumulated depreciation, and book value for each year under the straight-line method.

STRAIGHT-LINE DEPRECIATION

Apx. Exercise 2 (LO 2) SUM-OF-THE-YEARS'-DIGITS DEPRECIATION

Using the information given in Exercise 1, prepare a depreciation schedule showing the depreciation expense, accumulated depreciation, and book value for each year under the sum-of-the-years'-digits method.

SUM-OF-THE-YEARS'-DIGITS DEPRECIATION

Apx. Exercise 3 (LO 3) DOUBLE-DECLINING-BALANCE DEPRECIATION

Using the information given in Exercise 1, prepare a depreciation schedule showing the depreciation expense, accumulated depreciation, and book value for each year under the double-declining-balance method.

DOUBLE-DECLINING-BALANCE DEPRECIATION

Apx. Exercise 4 (LO 4) DEPRECIATION UNDER THE MODIFIED ACCELERATED COST RECOVERY SYSTEM

Using the information given in Exercise 1 and the rates shown in Figure 5A-4 of the text, prepare a depreciation schedule showing the depreciation expense, accumulated depreciation, and book value for each year under the Modified Accelerated Cost Recovery System. For tax purposes, assume that the office equipment has a useful life of 5 years. (The IRS schedule will spread depreciation over six years.)

MODIFIED ACCELERATED COST RECOVERY SYSTEM

CHAPTER 6
FINANCIAL STATEMENTS AND THE CLOSING PROCESS

LEARNING OBJECTIVES

Chapter 5 introduced the work sheet and demonstrated how it is used to prepare year-end adjustments. Chapter 6 completes the discussion of the work sheet by illustrating its role in the preparation of financial statements and closing entries. The purpose of the post-closing trial balance is also explained. It is prepared after closing entries have been posted to the general ledger accounts.

Objective 1.   Prepare financial statements with the aid of a work sheet.

The work sheet contains almost all information needed to prepare the income statement, the statement of owner's equity, and the balance sheet. Numbers can be taken directly from the Income Statement columns for the income statement. The owner's capital account must be reviewed before completing the statement of owner's equity. If additional investments were made, they must be added to the beginning capital balance to compute the total investment. The net income (or net loss) is added to the total investment, and withdrawals (drawing) are subtracted, giving the ending owner's equity. The balance sheet is prepared using the ending owner's equity balance reported on the statement of owner's equity and the permanent accounts listed in the Balance Sheet columns of the work sheet.

Objective 2.   Journalize and post closing entries.

After the work sheet is completed, the financial statements are prepared. Then the adjusting and closing entries are journalized and posted. All temporary accounts need zero balances to begin the new accounting period. The closing process has four journal entries:

1.   to close the revenue account(s) to Income Summary
2.   to close the expense accounts to Income Summary
3.   to close the Income Summary account to the capital account, and
4.   to close the Drawing account to the Capital account.

Objective 3.   Prepare a post-closing trial balance.

The **post-closing trial balance** lists all the permanent accounts that have balances to begin the new accounting period. It is prepared to prove the equality of the debit and credit balances in the general ledger accounts following the closing process. Since temporary accounts (drawing, revenues, and expenses) are closed at the end of the period, they do not appear on the post-closing trial balance.

Objective 4.   List and describe the steps in the accounting cycle.

This chapter concludes the accounting cycle that began in Chapter 1. The ten steps are

1.   analyze source documents
2.   journalize transactions
3.   post transactions to general ledger accounts
4.   prepare the trial balance (work sheet)
5.   determine and prepare needed adjustments (work sheet)
6.   complete the work sheet
7.   prepare the financial statements (income statement, statement of owner's equity, and balance sheet)

8.   journalize the adjusting and closing entries

9.   post the adjusting and closing entries, and

10.   prepare the post-closing trial balance.

REVIEW QUESTIONS

Instructions: Analyze each of the following items carefully before writing your answer in the column at the right.

Question	Answer
LO 1 1. The work sheet provides all of the needed information to prepare which three financial statements?.....................................	_____
LO 1 2. The income statement contains which two major types of accounts?	_____
LO 1 3. The statement of owner's equity adds _____ to the beginning owner's equity and subtracts _____.	_____
LO 1 4. Amounts owed that will be paid within a year are called _____.	_____
LO 1 5. Expenses are listed on the income statement in the order they appear on the chart of accounts or in descending order by _____ amount.	_____
LO 1 6. To find if the owner made any additional investments during the period, we must review the _____ account in the general ledger.	_____
LO 1 7. When net income and additional investments are greater than withdrawals, the difference is called a(n) _____ in capital for the month.	_____
LO 1 8. When the balance sheet is shown in _____ form, liabilities and owner's equity sections are placed below the assets section.	_____
LO 1 9. When the balance sheet is shown in _____ form, assets are on the left and liabilities and owner's equity are on the right.	_____
LO 1 10. A(n) _____ balance sheet groups similar items together such as current assets and current liabilities.	_____
LO 1 11. Cash and assets that will be converted to cash or consumed within a year or the normal operating cycle are called _____ assets. ...	_____
LO 1 12. The _____ is the period of time required to purchase supplies and services and convert them back into cash.	_____
LO 1 13. Accounts Payable and Wages Payable are classified as _____ Liabilities.	_____
LO 2 14. Assets, liabilities, and the owner's capital account accumulate information across accounting periods; they are called _____ accounts.	_____
LO 2 15. Revenue, expense, and drawing accounts accumulate information for the specific period only, then they go back to _____ balances.	_____

LO 2 16. Because revenue, expense, and drawing accounts are closed
each accounting period, they are called _____ accounts. .... _____

LO 2 17. The _____ account is used to summarize the effects of revenue
and expense accounts; it is then closed to the Capital account. .... _____

LO 2 18. When closing entries are posted to the general ledger, the word
_____ is written in the Item column of each general ledger
account affected. .... _____

LO 3 19. The _____ trial balance only lists permanent accounts. .... _____

LO 4 20. The _____ begins with analyzing source documents and ends
with the post-closing trial balance. .... _____

EXERCISES AND PROBLEMS

Exercise 1 (LO 1) REVIEW: COMPUTE NET INCOME

From the information given below, compute net income: _____

Revenue:	Delivery Fees	$4,826
Expenses:	Wages Expense	2,700
	Rent Expense	350
	Supplies Expense	55
	Insurance Expense	33
	Depreciation Expense	100

Exercise 2 (LO 1) REVIEW: COMPUTE OWNER'S EQUITY

Using the net income from Exercise 1 and the following information,   (a)_____
compute the (a) increase to owner's equity and (b) ending owner's equity
balance. Assume no additional investments were made by the owners.   (b)_____

Beginning Owner's Equity:	$5,680
Withdrawals by Owner:	1,000

Exercise 3 (LO 2) THE CLOSING PROCESS

Based upon Exercises 1 and 2 above, list the accounts that must be
closed at the end of the accounting cycle (in addition to the income
summary account).

_____

_____

_____

_____

_____

_____

_____

PROBLEMS

A completed work sheet for Collins Cycle Service as of April 30, 20— appears on pages 78–79. The general ledger is provided on pages 82–86.

Required:

From the work sheet on pages 78–79, complete the problems that follow.

Problem 4 (LO 1) PREPARE AN INCOME STATEMENT

Prepare the income statement.

Problem 4 (Continued)

COLLINS CYCLE

WORK

FOR MONTH ENDED

	DESCRIPTION	TRIAL BALANCE						ADJUSTMENTS							
		DEBIT				CREDIT			DEBIT				CREDIT			
1	Cash	4	8	0	0	00										
2	Supplies		8	2	6	00							(a)	3	2	6	00
3	Prepaid Insurance	1	3	0	0	00							(b)	2	0	0	00
4	Repair Equipment	2	6	0	0	00											
5	Accum. Depr.—Repair Equip.							4	0	0	00			(c)	4	0	0	00
6	Accounts Payable						1	3	0	0	00						
7	Wages Payable													(d)	1	0	0	00
8	Jean Collins, Capital						6	0	0	0	00						
9	Jean Collins, Drawing		3	0	0	00											
10	Repair Fees						2	8	3	9	00						
11	Wages Expense		2	7	5	00				(d)	1	0	0	00			
12	Rent Expense		4	0	0	00											
13	Supplies Expense									(a)	3	2	6	00			
14	Telephone Expense			3	8	00											
15	Insurance Expense									(b)	2	0	0	00			
16	Depreciation Exp.—Repair Equip.									(c)	4	0	0	00			
17		10	5	3	9	00	10	5	3	9	00	1	0	2	6	00	1	0	2	6	00
18	Net Income																
19																	

Problem 4 (Concluded)

SERVICE _____

SHEET _____

APRIL 30, 20--

ADJUSTED TRIAL BALANCE		INCOME STATEMENT		BALANCE SHEET		
DEBIT	CREDIT	DEBIT	CREDIT	DEBIT	CREDIT	
4 8 0 0 00				4 8 0 0 00		1
5 0 0 00				5 0 0 00		2
1 1 0 0 00				1 1 0 0 00		3
2 6 0 0 00				2 6 0 0 00		4
	8 0 0 00				8 0 0 00	5
	1 3 0 0 00				1 3 0 0 00	6
	1 0 0 00				1 0 0 00	7
	6 0 0 0 00				6 0 0 0 00	8
3 0 0 00				3 0 0 00		9
	2 8 3 9 00		2 8 3 9 00			10
3 7 5 00		3 7 5 00				11
4 0 0 00		4 0 0 00				12
3 2 6 00		3 2 6 00				13
3 8 00		3 8 00				14
2 0 0 00		2 0 0 00				15
4 0 0 00		4 0 0 00				16
11 0 3 9 00	11 0 3 9 00	1 7 3 9 00	2 8 3 9 00	9 3 0 0 00	8 2 0 0 00	17
		1 1 0 0 00			1 1 0 0 00	18
		2 8 3 9 00	2 8 3 9 00	9 3 0 0 00	9 3 0 0 00	19

Problem 5 (LO 2) PREPARE A STATEMENT OF OWNER'S EQUITY

Prepare the statement of owner's equity. Be sure to check the capital account in the general ledger.

_____

_____

_____

Problem 6 (LO 1) PREPARE A BALANCE SHEET

Problem 6 (LO 1) PREPARE A BALANCE SHEET

Prepare the balance sheet in report form.

Problem 7 REVIEW: PREPARE ADJUSTING ENTRIES

Journalize the adjusting entries and post them to the general ledger accounts. (Use the General Journal provided on page 81 for Problems 7 and 8.) The balances shown in the general ledger accounts are *Trial Balance* amounts—that is, before adjusting and closing entries are entered.

Problem 8 (LO 2) JOURNALIZING AND POSTING CLOSING ENTRIES

Journalize the closing entries and post them to the general ledger accounts.

Problems 7 and 8

GENERAL JOURNAL

PAGE 2

	DATE		DESCRIPTION	POST. REF.	DEBIT	CREDIT	
1							1
2							2
3							3
4							4
5							5
6							6
7							7
8							8
9							9
10							10
11							11
12							12
13							13
14							14
15							15
16							16
17							17
18							18
19							19
20							20
21							21
22							22
23							23
24							24
25							25
26							26
27							27
28							28
29							29
30							30
31							31
32							32
33							33

Problems 7 and 8 (Continued)

GENERAL LEDGER

ACCOUNT   Cash   ACCOUNT NO.   101

DATE		ITEM	POST. REF.	DEBIT	CREDIT	BALANCE	
						DEBIT	CREDIT
20— Apr.	30	Balance	√			4 8 0 0 00	

ACCOUNT   Supplies   ACCOUNT NO.   141

DATE		ITEM	POST. REF.	DEBIT	CREDIT	BALANCE	
						DEBIT	CREDIT
20— Apr.	30	Balance	√			8 2 6 00	

ACCOUNT   Prepaid Insurance   ACCOUNT NO.   145

DATE		ITEM	POST. REF.	DEBIT	CREDIT	BALANCE	
						DEBIT	CREDIT
20— Apr.	30	Balance	√			1 3 0 0 00	

ACCOUNT   Repair Equipment   ACCOUNT NO.   188

DATE		ITEM	POST. REF.	DEBIT	CREDIT	BALANCE	
						DEBIT	CREDIT
20— Apr.	30	Balance	√			2 6 0 0 00	

Problems 7 and 8 (Continued)

ACCOUNT Accumulated Depreciation—Repair Equipment ACCOUNT NO. 188.1

DATE		ITEM	POST. REF.	DEBIT	CREDIT	BALANCE	
						DEBIT	CREDIT
20— Apr.	1	Balance	√				4 0 0 00

ACCOUNT Accounts Payable ACCOUNT NO. 202

DATE		ITEM	POST. REF.	DEBIT	CREDIT	BALANCE	
						DEBIT	CREDIT
20— Apr.	30	Balance	√				1 3 0 0 00

ACCOUNT Wages Payable ACCOUNT NO. 219

DATE		ITEM	POST. REF.	DEBIT	CREDIT	BALANCE	
						DEBIT	CREDIT

ACCOUNT Jean Collins, Capital ACCOUNT NO. 311

DATE		ITEM	POST. REF.	DEBIT	CREDIT	BALANCE	
						DEBIT	CREDIT
20— Apr.	1	Balance	√				5 0 0 0 00
	15		J1		1 0 0 0 00		6 0 0 0 00

Problems 7 and 8 (Continued)

ACCOUNT   Jean Collins, Drawing   ACCOUNT NO.   312

DATE		ITEM	POST. REF.	DEBIT	CREDIT	BALANCE	
						DEBIT	CREDIT
20— Apr.	30	Balance	√			3 0 0 00	

ACCOUNT   Income Summary   ACCOUNT NO.   313

DATE		ITEM	POST. REF.	DEBIT	CREDIT	BALANCE	
						DEBIT	CREDIT

ACCOUNT   Repair Fees   ACCOUNT NO.   401

DATE		ITEM	POST. REF.	DEBIT	CREDIT	BALANCE	
						DEBIT	CREDIT
20— Apr.	30	Balance	√				2 8 3 9 00

ACCOUNT   Wages Expense   ACCOUNT NO.   511

DATE		ITEM	POST. REF.	DEBIT	CREDIT	BALANCE	
						DEBIT	CREDIT
20— Apr.	30	Balance	√			2 7 5 00	

Problems 7 and 8 (Continued)

ACCOUNT Rent Expense   ACCOUNT NO. 521

DATE		ITEM	POST. REF.	DEBIT	CREDIT	BALANCE	
						DEBIT	CREDIT
20— Apr.	30	Balance	√			4 0 0 00	

ACCOUNT Supplies Expense   ACCOUNT NO. 524

DATE		ITEM	POST. REF.	DEBIT	CREDIT	BALANCE	
						DEBIT	CREDIT

ACCOUNT Telephone Expense   ACCOUNT NO. 525

DATE		ITEM	POST. REF.	DEBIT	CREDIT	BALANCE	
						DEBIT	CREDIT
20— Apr.	30	Balance	√			3 8 00	

ACCOUNT Insurance Expense   ACCOUNT NO. 535

DATE		ITEM	POST. REF.	DEBIT	CREDIT	BALANCE	
						DEBIT	CREDIT

Problems 7 and 8 (Concluded)

ACCOUNT   Depreciation Expense—Repair Equipment   ACCOUNT NO.   542

DATE		ITEM	POST. REF.	DEBIT	CREDIT	BALANCE	
						DEBIT	CREDIT

Problem 9 (LO 3) PREPARE A POST-CLOSING TRIAL BALANCE

Prepare the post-closing trial balance.

ACCOUNT	ACCT. NO.	DEBIT BALANCE	CREDIT BALANCE

CHAPTER 6 APPENDIX
STATEMENT OF CASH FLOWS

APPENDIX LEARNING OBJECTIVES

In Chapter 6, we reviewed in greater detail the preparation of three financial statements: the income statement, statement of owner's equity, and balance sheet. A fourth important financial statement is the statement of cash flows. The main purpose of this statement is to report the sources and uses of cash. These sources and uses are categorized into three types of business activities: operating, investing, and financing.

Objective 1.   Categorize business transactions as operating, investing, or financing.

Operating activities include those cash flows that are related to the revenues and expenses reported on the income statement. Examples include cash received for services performed and the payment of cash for expenses.

Investing activities are those transactions associated with buying and selling long-term assets, lending money, and collecting the principal on the related loans.

Financing activities are those cash transactions with owners and creditors. Examples include cash received from the owner to finance the operations and cash paid to the owner as withdrawals. Financing activities also include the receipt of cash from loans and the repayment of the loans.

Objective 2.   Prepare a statement of cash flows by analyzing and categorizing a series of business transactions.

The main body of the statement of cash flows consists of three sections: operating, investing, and financing activities.

Name of Business
Statement of Cash Flows
For Period Ended Date

Cash flows from operating activities:
Cash received from customers $ x,xxx
List cash paid for various
    expenses $ (xxx)
   Total cash paid for operations   (x,xxx)
   Net cash provided by (used
    for) operating activities $ xxx

Cash flows from investing activities:
List cash received from the
    sale of long-term assets
    and other investing
    activities $ x,xxx

List cash paid for the purchase
    of long-term assets
    and other investing
    activities   <u>(x,xxx)</u>
    Net cash provided by (used
       for) investing activities   (x,xxx)
Cash flows from financing activities:
    List cash received from
       owners and creditors $ x,xxx
    List cash paid to owners and
       creditors   <u>(xxx)</u>
      Net cash provided by (used
       for) financing activities   <u>x,xxx</u>
Net increase (decrease) in cash   <u>$ xxx</u>

Apx. Exercise 1 REVIEW: ENTERING TRANSACTIONS IN T-ACCOUNTS

Sung Joon Lee opened an overseas mailing business, "Lee's Quick Sail." The following transactions occurred during August of the current year. Enter the transactions in the Cash T account provided below, identifying each with its corresponding letter.

(a)   Lee invested $5,000 in the business.

(b)   Paid office rent, $500.

(c)   Bought supplies for the month, $200.

(d)   Lee made an additional investment in the business, $1,000.

(e)   Bought a new scale for $1,200: $700 cash and $500 on account.

(f)   Received $600 for mailing services.

(g)   Paid $200 on loan (see transaction (e)).

(h)   Paid electricity bill, $64.

(i)   Paid gas bill, $70.

(j)   Received $900 for mailing services.

(k)   Paid part-time employee, $90.

(l)   Lee withdrew cash for personal use, $400.

CASH

Apx. Exercise 2 REVIEW: FOOTING AND BALANCING A T-ACCOUNT

Foot and balance the T account in Exercise 1. The cash balance at the end of August is _____ .

Problem 3 (LO 1) CLASSIFYING BUSINESS TRANSACTIONS AS OPERATING, INVESTING, OR FINANCING

Label each transaction in the Cash T account of Exercise 1 as an operating (O), investing (I), or financing (F) activity.

Problem 4 (LO 2) PREPARING A STATEMENT OF CASH FLOWS BY ANALYZING BUSINESS TRANSACTIONS.

Prepare a statement of cash flows based on the transactions and Cash T account in Exercises 1 through 2 and Problem 3.

CHAPTER 7
ACCOUNTING FOR CASH

LEARNING OBJECTIVES

Managing cash is an essential part of every business's operations. In Chapter 7, we explore the cash account—setting up a bank account, writing checks and making deposits, preparing a bank reconciliation and the journal entries needed, operating a petty cash fund, establishing a change fund and using a cash short and over account.

Objective 1.   Describe how to open and use a checking account.

Most banks have standard procedures for opening and using a **checking account.** They begin with a signature card, whereby the depositor's social security number or EIN number and signature are provided. Preparing deposit tickets, endorsing properly, and writing checks, are parts of using a checking account wisely.

Objective 2.   Prepare a bank reconciliation and related journal entries.

On a monthly basis, banks send **bank statements** to their checking account customers. The bank statement must be reconciled—compared to the checkbook. Adjustments are made to the ending bank balance and the checkbook balance until they are equal. Once the bank reconciliation is prepared, any changes to the book (checkbook) balance will require journal entries.

Objective 3.   Establish and use a petty cash fund.

A **petty cash fund** is both convenient and cost-effective. Rather than writing checks for small amounts, costing time and money, a sum of money is set aside for petty (small) cash payments during the month. Vouchers are issued for all money paid out; the petty cash fund is replenished at the end of the month (brought back up to its original amount). A journal entry is made to record all of the expenses shown in the petty cash record.

Objective 4.   Establish a change fund and use the cash short and over account.

Businesses that receive cash from customers generally need to establish a change fund of currency and coins to use in handling cash sales. When many cash transactions occur, there often will be a difference between what the cash register tape says and the amount of cash actually found in the drawer. An account called Cash Short and Over is used to account for these differences. At the end of the month, if there is more cash short than over, it is an expense to the business. If there is more cash over than short, it is a revenue to the business.

REVIEW QUESTIONS

Instructions: Analyze each of the following carefully before writing your answer in the column at the right.

	Question	**Answer**

LO 1 **1.** To open a checking account, each person authorized to sign checks must fill out a(n) _____. .... _____

LO 1 **2.** A(n) _____ lists items being deposited to a checking account. .... _____

LO 1 **3.** Each check deposited is identified by its _____. .... _____

LO 1 **4.** A(n) _____ consists of stamping or writing the depositor's name and other information on the back of a check. .... _____

LO 1 **5.** A(n) _____ endorsement consists of a signature on the back of a check. .... _____

LO 1 **6.** A(n) _____ endorsement consists of a signature together with words such as "For Deposit." .... _____

LO 1 **7.** Depositors using ATM machines must first key in their _____. ... _____

LO 1 **8.** A(n) _____ is a document ordering a bank to pay cash from the depositor's account. .... _____

LO 1 **9.** The _____ is the bank on which a check is drawn. .... _____

LO 1 **10.** The _____ is the person being paid the cash. .... _____

LO 1 **11.** The _____ is the depositor who orders the bank to pay the cash. _____

LO 1 **12.** Space is contained to record all relevant information about a check on its _____. .... _____

LO 1 **13.** A statement issued to the depositor once a month is called a _____. .... _____

LO 1 **14.** Checks paid by the bank and returned to the depositor are called _____. .... _____

LO 2 **15.** The process of bringing the bank and book balances into agreement is called preparing a(n) .... _____

LO 2 **16.** Checks issued during the period but not yet processed by the bank are called _____. .... _____

LO 2 **17.** Deposits made but not yet recorded by the bank are called _____. _____

LO 2 **18.** Bank charges for services are called _____. .... _____

LO 2 **19.** Checks deposited but not paid because the drawer did not have enough money in the account are called _____ checks. .... _____

LO 2 **20.** Transactions can be completed by _____ rather than by the manual process of writing checks or using cash. .... _____

LO 3 **21.** A fund called _____ is established to pay for small items with cash. .... _____

LO 3 22. A receipt called a(n) _____ is prepared for every payment from the petty cash fund. .... _____

LO 3 23. The _____ is a special multi-column record where petty cash payments are recorded. .... _____

LO 3 24. At the end of the month, the petty cash fund is _____, or brought up to its original amount. .... _____

LO 4 25. The cash short and over account is used when actual cash on hand is different from what is on the _____ tape plus the change fund. _____

LO 4 26. When actual cash on hand exceeds what is on the register tape plus the change fund, this difference is a(n) _____. .... _____

LO 4 27. When actual cash on hand is less than what is on the register tape plus the change fund, this difference is a(n) _____. .... _____

EXERCISES AND PROBLEMS

Exercise 1 (LO1) PREPARE DEPOSIT TICKET

Using the deposit ticket shown below, enter the following information:

Date:	March 28, 20—	Checks:	33-11	$202.00
Currency:	$318.00		123-666	48.00
Coin:	33.00		2-9	211.00

PEOPLE'S BANK
Wilkes-Barre, PA 18704-1456

Date _____ 20 _____

CHECKS AND OTHER ITEMS ARE RECEIVED FOR DEPOSIT SUBJECT TO THE TERMS AND CONDITIONS OF THIS FINANCIAL INSTITUTION'S ACCOUNT AGREEMENT.

SIGN HERE ONLY IF CASH RECEIVED FROM DEPOSIT

⑆063112094⑆ 0001632475⑈

DEPOSIT TICKET

CURRENCY		
COIN		
CHECKS		
TOTAL FROM OTHER SIDE		
SUBTOTAL		
LESS CASH RECEIVED		
NET DEPOSIT		

Exercise 2 (LO1) PREPARE CHECK AND STUB

During the month of October, you made the following payments by check. Fill in the stubs and write the checks. Use the blank checks provided on page 94. Enter $825.50 as the balance brought forward on Check No. 138, and add a deposit for $85 on October 10.

Oct. 3   Issued Check No. 138 to Emerald Lawn Care, Inc. for work done on the shrubbery around the office building, $125.00. (Miscellaneous Expense)

8   Issued Check No. 139 to Maxwell Office Supply for stationery, $85.90. (Office Supplies)

10   Issued Check No. 140 to Wesley's Towing for cost of towing company car to repair shop, for $50.00. (Automobile Expense)

Exercise 2 (Continued)

No. 138

DATE _____ 20 _____
TO _____
FOR _____
_____

ACCT. _____

	DOLLARS	CENTS
BAL BRO'T FOR'D		
AMT. DEPOSITED		
TOTAL		
AMT. THIS CHECK		
BAL CAR'D FOR'D		

No. 138   60-55/313

_____ 20 _____

PAY
TO THE
ORDER OF _____ $ _____

_____ Dollars

FOR CLASSROOM USE ONLY

PEOPLE'S BANK
Wilkes-Barre, PA 18704-1456

MEMO _____ BY _____

⑉1300555 16 3247 5⑈

No. 139

DATE _____ 20 _____
TO _____
FOR _____
_____

ACCT. _____

	DOLLARS	CENTS
BAL BRO'T FOR'D		
AMT. DEPOSITED		
TOTAL		
AMT. THIS CHECK		
BAL CAR'D FOR'D		

No. 139   60-55/313

_____ 20 _____

PAY
TO THE
ORDER OF _____ $ _____

_____ Dollars

FOR CLASSROOM USE ONLY

PEOPLE'S BANK
Wilkes-Barre, PA 18704-1456

MEMO _____ BY _____

⑉1300555 16 3247 5⑈

No. 140

DATE _____ 20 _____
TO _____
FOR _____
_____

ACCT. _____

	DOLLARS	CENTS
BAL BRO'T FOR'D		
AMT. DEPOSITED		
TOTAL		
AMT. THIS CHECK		
BAL CAR'D FOR'D		

No. 140   60-55/313

_____ 20 _____

PAY
TO THE
ORDER OF _____ $ _____

_____ Dollars

FOR CLASSROOM USE ONLY

PEOPLE'S BANK
Wilkes-Barre, PA 18704-1456

MEMO _____ BY _____

⑉1300555 16 3247 5⑈

Exercise 3 (LO2) BANK RECONCILIATION PROCEDURES

The bank reconciliation is a process of matching the checkbook balance with the bank statement balance—adding and subtracting items until the two are equal. In the exercise below, indicate which action is taken:

    a.   Add to checkbook balance.

    b.   Subtract from checkbook balance.

    c.   Add to bank statement balance.

    d.   Subtract from bank statement balance.

_____   1.   Deposits in transit

_____   2.   Error in checkbook whereby a check for $128 was entered into the checkbook as $182

_____   3.   NSF check

_____   4.   Checks outstanding (not yet processed by the bank)

_____   5.   Bank service fees

_____   6.   Credit memo, telling depositor that a note was collected

_____   7.   Error in checkbook whereby a check for $181 was entered into the checkbook as $118

Exercise 4 (LO 2) PREPARE JOURNAL ENTRIES FOR BANK RECONCILIATION

Based on the following bank reconciliation, prepare the necessary journal entries as of January 28, 20—:

Bank statement balance, January 28		$1,896.00
Add: Deposits in transit:		
1/26	$118.00	
1/28	92.00	210.00
		$2,106.00
Deduct: Outstanding checks:		
No. 683	$ 23.00	
No. 685	6.50	
No. 687	102.50	
No. 688	13.00	
No. 689	208.00	353.00
Adjusted bank balance		$1,753.00
Book balance, January 28		$1,994.00
Add: Error on check*	$ 28.00	
Note collected**	142.00	170.00
		$2,164.00
Deduct: Unrecorded ATM withdrawal***	$ 30.00	
Service charge	11.00	
NSF check	370.00	411.00
Adjusted book balance		$1,753.00

*   Accounts Payable was debited.
**   Credit Notes Receivable.
***   Debit Gail Bennett, Drawing

Exercise 4 (Concluded)

GENERAL JOURNAL   PAGE

	DATE		DESCRIPTION	POST. REF.	DEBIT	CREDIT	
1							1
2							2
3							3
4							4
5							5
6							6
7							7
8							8
9							9
10							10
11							11
12							12
13							13
14							14
15							15
16							16
17							17
18							18
19							19
20							20
21							21
22							22

Exercise 5 (LO3) PETTY CASH JOURNAL ENTRIES

Based on the following petty cash information, prepare journal entries to establish the petty cash fund and to replenish the fund at the end of the month.

1. On March 1, a check is written for $100 to establish a petty cash fund.

2. During the month, the following petty cash payments are made:

Telephone Expense	$ 3.50
Automobile Expense	11.00
Postage Expense	4.50
B. Crenshaw, Drawing	35.00
Charitable Contributions Expense	25.00
Miscellaneous Expense	3.00

Exercise 5 (Concluded)

GENERAL JOURNAL   PAGE 1

	DATE	DESCRIPTION	POST. REF.	DEBIT	CREDIT	
1						1
2						2
3						3
4						4
5						5
6						6
7						7
8						8
9						9
10						10
11						11
12						12
13						13
14						14
15						15
16						16
17						17
18						18
19						19
20						20
21						21
22						22
23						23
24						

Exercise 6 (LO4) CASH SHORT AND OVER JOURNAL ENTRIES

Based on the following information, prepare weekly entries for cash receipts from service fees and cash short and over. A change fund of $100 is maintained.

August	5	Cash in drawer:	$318.00	Cash register amount:	$ 218.00
	12		402.00		300.00
	19		388.00		292.00
	26		411.50		309.50

Exercise 6 (Concluded)

GENERAL JOURNAL   PAGE 1

	DATE		DESCRIPTION	POST. REF.	DEBIT	CREDIT	
1							1
2							2
3							3
4							4
5							5
6							6
7							7
8							8
9							9
10							10
11							11
12							12
13							13
14							14
15							15
16							16
17							17
18							18
19							19
20							20
21							21
22							22
23							23
24							24
25							25
26							26
27							27
28							28

Problem 7 (LO2) BANK RECONCILIATION AND RELATED JOURNAL ENTRIES

The following information relates to the bank account of the Mini Donut House:

Balance, March 31, per check stub		$2,923.00
Balance, March 31, per bank statement		3,199.00
March deposits not shown on bank statement	$302.00	
	206.00	508.00
Bank service charge shown on bank statement		14.00
Unrecorded ATM withdrawal*		60.00
NSF check shown on bank statement		153.00

Error on Check 144, where stub shows $132.00, but the check was made in the amount of $123.00. Accounts Payable was originally debited.

Checks outstanding, March 31:
No. 148	$201.00
No. 151	300.00
No. 155	501.00

*Funds were withdrawn by the owner, Paolo Goes, for personal use.

Required:

1. Prepare the bank reconciliation.
2. Prepare the required journal entries.

Problem 7 (Continued)

1.

Problem 7 (Concluded)

2.

GENERAL JOURNAL   PAGE 1

	DATE		DESCRIPTION	POST. REF.	DEBIT	CREDIT	
1							1
2							2
3							3
4							4
5							5
6							6
7							7
8							8
9							9
10							10
11							11
12							12
13							13
14							14
15							15
16							16
17							17
18							18
19							19
20							20
21							21
22							22
23							23
24							24
25							25
26							26
27							27
28							28
29							29

Problem 8 (LO3) PETTY CASH PAYMENTS RECORD AND JOURNAL ENTRIES

On April 1, the Fitzgibbons Furniture Repair Shop established a petty cash fund of $200.00. The following cash payments were made from the petty cash fund during the first two weeks of April. The fund was replenished to the $200.00 level on April 16.

April   1   Paid $5.28 for postage due on a package received. Petty Cash Voucher No. 10.

          5   Made a $25.00 contribution to the Washington Township Baseball League. Petty Cash Voucher No. 11.

          6   Reimbursed $6.25 to an employee for phone calls made from a pay telephone. Petty Cash Voucher No. 12.

          8   Paid $22.00 for office supplies. Petty Cash Voucher No. 13.

        10   Paid $32.00 for a newspaper advertisement. Petty Cash Voucher No. 14.

        12   Paid $33.00 for gas and an oil change for the company truck. Petty Cash Voucher No. 15.

        14   Paid $20.00 for postage stamps. Petty Cash Voucher No. 16.

        15   Made a $25.00 contribution to the Girl Scouts, Petty Cash Voucher No. 17.

Required:

1. Prepare the journal entry to establish the petty cash fund.
2. Enter the above payments in the petty cash payments record provided on page 103.
3. Prove the petty cash payments record.
4. Prepare the journal entry to replenish the fund on April 16.

Problem 8 (Continued)

PETTY CASH PAYMENTS FOR MONTH OF

20--   PAGE 1

DAY	DESCRIPTION	VOU. NO.	TOTAL AMOUNT	TRUCK EXPENSE	POSTAGE EXPENSE	CHARIT. CONTRIB. EXPENSE	TEL. EXPENSE	OFFICE SUPPLIES	ADVER. EXPENSE	ACCOUNT	AMOUNT
										DISTRIBUTION OF PAYMENTS	
1											
2											
3											
4											
5											
6											
7											
8											
9											
10											
11											
12											
13											
14											
15											
16											
17											
18											
19											
20											
21											
22											

Problem 8 (Concluded)

GENERAL JOURNAL   PAGE 1

	DATE		DESCRIPTION	POST REF.	DEBIT	CREDIT	
1							1
2							2
3							3
4							4
5							5
6							6
7							7
8							8
9							9
10							10
11							11
12							12
13							13
14							14
15							15
16							16
17							17
18							18
19							19
20							20
21							21

Problem 9 (LO4) CASH SHORT AND OVER JOURNAL ENTRIES

Mackie's Salon deposits cash weekly. A record of cash register receipts for the month of April is shown below. A change fund of $100 is maintained.

April	2	Cash in drawer:	$298.00	Cash register amount:	$ 196.50
	9		286.50		192.00
	16		293.50		193.50
	23		306.00		204.50
	30		301.50		203.00

Required:

Prepare weekly journal entries for cash receipts from service fees, showing cash short and over when needed.

Problem 9 (Concluded)

GENERAL JOURNAL   PAGE 1

	DATE		DESCRIPTION	POST REF.	DEBIT	CREDIT	
1							1
2							2
3							3
4							4
5							5
6							6
7							7
8							8
9							9
10							10
11							11
12							12
13							13
14							14
15							15
16							16
17							17
18							18
19							19
20							20
21							21
22							22
23							23
24							24
25							25
26							26
27							27
28							28
29							29
30							30
31							31
32							32

CHAPTER 8
PAYROLL ACCOUNTING:
EMPLOYEE EARNINGS AND DEDUCTIONS

LEARNING OBJECTIVES

Payroll accounting is an important part of any business, partly because it is such a significant expense and partly because so many laws govern its record keeping. In Chapter 8, we examine the payroll records that employers are required to keep and also those records that are maintained for administrative efficiency.

Objective 1.   Distinguish between employees and independent contractors.

An **employee** is one who works under the control and direction of an employer. The employer controls how and when the job is to be done, determines working hours, and in general is responsible for all aspects of the employee's work. An **independent contractor**, on the other hand, performs a service for a fee and does not work under the control and direction of the company paying for his or her service. This is an important distinction because employers are required to maintain payroll records and file many reports for their employees but must file only one form for independent contractors.

Objective 2.   Calculate employee earnings and deductions.

Three steps are required to determine how much to pay an employee for a pay period. Calculate the employee's total earnings for the pay period, determine the amounts of deductions for the same pay period, and subtract deductions from total earnings. The deductions may be required by law—for example, Social Security and Medicare taxes and federal and state income taxes—or by agreement with the employer—for example, insurance deductions and savings bond deductions.

Objective 3.   Describe and prepare payroll records.

Three types of payroll records are used to accumulate required information for federal and state tax purposes. The payroll register, the payroll check with earnings statement attached, and the employee earnings record.

The **payroll register** is a multi-column form that accumulates the necessary data to prepare the journal entry. Detailed information on earnings, taxable earnings, deductions, and net pay is provided for each employee and for the employees in total.

The **payroll check** is prepared from information in the payroll register. The detachable earnings statement attached to the employee's check shows the gross earnings, total deductions, and net pay.

A separate record of each employee's earnings is called an **employee earnings record.** This information is also obtained from the payroll register. The earnings record is designed so that quarterly and annual totals can be accumulated in order for the employer to prepare several reports.

Objective 4.   Account for employee earnings and deductions.

The payroll register provides all the information needed to prepare the journal entry for any pay period. The total gross earnings is debited to a wages and salaries expense account, and each deduction is credited to a current liability account. The difference between gross earnings and total deductions is called **net pay** and is credited to cash.

Objective 5.   Describe various payroll record-keeping methods.

In addition to a manual system of preparing all the necessary payroll records, payroll processing centers and electronic systems can be used to prepare the same records.

A **payroll processing center** is a business that sells payroll record-keeping services. An **electronic system** is a computer system based on a software package that performs all payroll record keeping and prepares payroll checks.

REVIEW QUESTIONS

Instructions: Analyze each of the following carefully before writing your answer in the column at the right.

Question	Answer

LO 1   1. A(n) _____ is one who works under the control and direction of an employer. ....   _____

LO 1   2. A(n) _____ performs a service for a fee and does not work under the control and direction of the company paying for the service. ....   _____

LO 2   3. What three steps are required to determine how much to pay an employee for a pay period? ....   _____

_____

_____

LO 2   4. Compensation for managerial or administrative services, normally expressed in biweekly, monthly, or annual terms, is called _____.   _____

LO 2   5. Compensation for skilled or unskilled labor, normally expressed in terms of hours, weeks, or units produced, is called _____. ....   _____

LO 2   6. When compensation is based on time, _____ are helpful for keeping a record of the time worked by each employee. ....   _____

LO 2   7. An employee's total earnings is also called _____. ....   _____

LO 2   8. An employee's total earnings less all the deductions is called _____.   _____

LO 2   9. What are the three major categories of deductions from an employee's paycheck?...   _____

_____

_____

LO 2   10. David Astin is married with two children, holds only one job, and has a spouse who is not employed. What number of withholding allowances is Astin entitled to claim, assuming that he does not anticipate large itemized deductions?..   _____

LO 2 11. Upon employment, each employee is required to furnish the employer a Form _____ that details, among other things, the number of withholding allowances and marital status.......................................   _____

LO 2 12. Name the four factors that determine the amount to be withheld from an employee's gross pay each pay period. ....   _____

_____

_____

_____

LO 3 13. A form used to assemble the data required at the end of each payroll period is called a(n) _____...   _____

LO 3 14. A method of payment in which the employee's net pay is placed directly in the employee's bank account is called a(n) _____.......   _____

LO 3 15. A separate, detailed record of each employee's earnings is called a(n) _____ ....   _____

LO 5 16. Name two approaches in addition to a manual system used to accumulate and record payroll information. ....   _____

_____

EXERCISES AND PROBLEMS

Exercise 1 (LO 2) COMPUTING OVERTIME PAY RATE

Lu-yin Cheng receives a regular salary of $2,500 a month and is entitled to overtime pay at the rate of one and one-half times the regular hourly rate for any time worked in excess of 40 hours per week. Compute Cheng's overtime hourly rate.

_____

_____

_____

_____

_____

_____

_____

_____

_____

_____

Exercise 2 (LO 2) COMPUTING GROSS PAY

Roger Watkins earns a regular hourly rate of $12.50 and receives time and a half for any time worked over 8 hours per weekday. Roger earns double time for hours worked on Saturday or Sunday. During the past week, Roger worked 8 hours each day Monday through Wednesday, 5 hours on Thursday, 12 hours on Friday, and 6 hours on Saturday. Compute Watkins's gross pay.

_____

_____

_____

_____

_____

_____

_____

_____

_____

Exercise 3 (LO 2) COMPUTING NET PAY

Bill Burry is married, has 3 children, and claims 5 withholding allowances for federal income tax purposes. Burry's gross pay for the week was $683.00. Using the federal income tax withholding table provided in Figure 8–4 of the text and the information provided below, compute Burry's net pay for the week.

(a)   Social Security tax rate is 6.2% (Burry's prior earnings equaled $23,455.00).
(b)   Medicare tax rate is 1.45%.
(c)   State income tax is 2% of gross earnings.
(d)   City income tax is 1% of gross earnings.
(e)   Contribution to pension plan is $25.00.
(f)   Health insurance deduction is $8.50.

_____

_____

_____

_____

_____

_____

_____

_____

_____

_____

Exercise 4 (LO 4) JOURNALIZING PAYROLL TRANSACTIONS

Using the information provided in Exercise 3, enter the payment of Bill Burry's wages in a general journal. Assume a pay period ending on July 31, 20—.

GENERAL JOURNAL   PAGE 1

	DATE	DESCRIPTION	POST. REF.	DEBIT	CREDIT	
1						1
2						2
3						3
4						4
5						5
6						6
7						7
8						8
9						9
10						10
11						11
12						12
13						13
14						14
15						15
16						16
17						17
18						18
19						19
20						20
21						21
22						22
23						23
24						24
25						25
26						26
27						27
28						28

Exercise 5 (LO 3, 4) PAYROLL JOURNAL ENTRIES

The following data were taken from the payroll register of United Processors as of 5/14/20--.

Regular earnings	$6,516.00
Overtime earnings	710.00
Total earnings	_____
Deductions:	
Federal income tax	_____
Social security tax	448.01
Medicare tax	104.78
Pension plan	134.00
Health insurance	260.00
United Way	190.00
Net pay	$5,394.21

Required:

1. Determine the missing amounts.
2. Prepare the journal entry for the payroll, crediting Cash for the net pay.

1.

_____

_____

_____

_____

2.

GENERAL JOURNAL   PAGE

	DATE		DESCRIPTION	POST. REF.	DEBIT	CREDIT	
1							1
2							2
3							3
4							4
5							5
6							6
7							7
8							8
9							9
10							10
11							11
12							12

Problem 6 (LO 2, 3, 4) PAYROLL REGISTER AND PAYROLL JOURNAL ENTRIES

Earl Wilson operates a business known as Wilson Enterprises. Listed below are the name, number of allowances claimed, marital status, total hours worked, and hourly rate of each employee. All hours worked in excess of 40 a week are paid for at the rate of time and a half.

The employer uses a weekly federal income tax withholding table. A portion of this weekly table is provided in Chapter 8 of your textbook. For White, Federal Income tax is $92.00. (This amount is not provided in the chapter table.) Social Security tax is withheld at the rate of 6.2%, Medicare tax is withheld at the rate of 1.45%, state income tax is withheld at the rate of 3.5%, and city earnings tax is withheld at the rate of 1%. O'Connor, Perez, Scalia, and Stephens each have $15.00 withheld this payday for group life insurance. Each employee, except Marshall, has $5.00 withheld for health insurance. All of the employees use payroll deduction to the credit union for varying amounts as listed below. Bertucci, Perez, and White each have $18.25 withheld this payday under a savings bond purchase plan.

Wilson Enterprises follows the practice of drawing a single check for the net amount of the payroll and depositing the check in a special payroll account at the bank. Individual paychecks are then drawn for the amount due each employee. The checks issued this payday were numbered consecutively beginning with No. 531.

Wilson Enterprises
Payroll Information for the Week Ended January 15, 20—

Name	Allow-ances	Marital Status	Total Hours Worked	Regular Hourly Rate	Credit Union Deposit	Cumul. Earnings thru 1/8
Bertucci, Harry	3	M	45	$12.00	$114.00	$525.00
Brennan, Joyce	4	M	50	10.00	110.00	480.00
Marshall, Teddy	5	M	43	11.00	97.90	500.00
O'Connor, Sandra	2	S	48	11.00	114.40	625.00
Perez, Lucy	3	M	43	13.00	115.70	730.00
Rehnquist, Willie	5	M	40	17.00	136.00	850.00
Scalia, Tonya	2	S	38	9.00	68.40	425.00
Stephens, J.P.	6	M	47	11.00	111.10	635.00
White, Byran	1	S	60	10.00	140.00	615.00

Required:

1. Prepare a payroll register for Wilson Enterprises for the pay period ended January 15, 20—. Use the form provided on pages 114–115. (In the Taxable Earnings/Unemployment Compensation column, enter the same amounts as in the Social Security column.)

2. Assuming that the wages for the week ended January 15 were paid on January 17, enter the payment in the general journal provided on page 115.

Problem 6 (Continued)

PAYROLL REGISTER

	NAME	EMP. NO.	NO. ALLOW.	MARIT. STATUS	EARNINGS							TAXABLE EARNINGS			
					REGULAR		OVERTIME		TOTAL		CUMULATIVE TOTAL		UNEMPLOY. COMP.		SOCIAL SECURITY	
1																
2																
3																
4																
5																
6																
7																
8																
9																
10																
11																

Problem 6 (Continued)

FOR PERIOD ENDED   20--

FEDERAL INC. TAX	SOC. SEC. TAX	MEDICARE TAX	STATE INC. TAX	CITY EARN. TAX	LIFE INS.	HEALTH INS.	CREDIT UNION	OTHER	TOTAL	NET PAY	CK. NO.	
												1
												2
												3
												4
												5
												6
												7
												8
												9
												10
												11

GENERAL JOURNAL   PAGE 1

	DATE	DESCRIPTION	POST. REF.	DEBIT	CREDIT	
1						1
2						2
3						3
4						4
5						5
6						6
7						7
8						8
9						9
10						10
11						11
12						12
13						13
14						14
15						15
16						16
17						17
18						18

Problem 7 (LO 3) EMPLOYEE EARNINGS RECORD

The current employee earnings record for Joyce Brennan is provided below and on page 117. Using the information provided in Problem 6, update Brennan's earnings record to reflect the January 15 payroll. Although this information should have been entered earlier, complete the required information at the bottom of the earnings record. The necessary information is provided below.

Name:	Joyce W. Brennan
Address:	422 Long Plain Rd.
	Leverett, MA 01054
Employee No.:	2
Gender:	Female
Department:	Sanitation
Occupation:	Janitor
S.S. No.:	336-56-7534
Marital Status:	Married
Allowances:	4
Pay Rate:	$10.00 per hour
Birth Date:	7/6/69
Date Employed:	6/22/--

EMPLOYEE EARNINGS RECORD

	20 -- PERIOD ENDED	EARNINGS					TAXABLE EARNINGS				DEDUCTIONS			
		REGULAR		OVERTIME		TOTAL	CUMULATIVE TOTAL	UNEMPLOY. COMP.		SOCIAL SECURITY		FEDERAL INCOME TAX		SOCIAL SECURITY TAX
1	Jan 1	200	00			200 00	200 00	200	00	200	00	0 00		12 40
2	Jan 8	280	00			280 00	480 00	280	00	280	00	0 00		17 36
3														
4														
5														
	GENDER	DEPARTMENT		OCCUPATION				SOCIAL SECURITY NO.				MARITAL STATUS		ALLOW- ANCES
	M F													

Problem 7 (Concluded)

FOR PERIOD ENDED   20--

MEDICARE TAX		STATE INCOME TAX		CITY EARNINGS TAX		LIFE INSUR		HEALTH INSUR.		CREDIT UNION		OTHER		TOTAL		NET PAY		CK. NO.	
												DEDUCTIONS							
2	90	7	00	2	00			5	00	40	00			69	30	130	70	321	1
4	06	9	80	2	80			5	00	56	00			95	02	184	98	422	2
																			3
																			4
																			5
																			6
																			7

PAY RATE	DATE OF BIRTH	DATE HIRED	NAME/ADDRESS	EMP. NO.

CHAPTER 9
PAYROLL ACCOUNTING:
EMPLOYER TAXES AND REPORTS

LEARNING OBJECTIVES

Chapter 8 discussed taxes levied on the employee and withheld by the employer. None of these taxes was an expense of the employer. In Chapter 9, we examine several taxes that represent an additional payroll expense imposed directly on the employer.

Objective 1.   Describe and calculate employer payroll taxes.

Most employers are subject to a matching portion of the Social Security and Medicare taxes and to federal and state unemployment taxes. The employer's **Social Security and Medicare taxes** are levied on employers at the same rates and on the same bases as the employee Social Security and Medicare taxes. The **FUTA** tax is levied only on employers. The purpose of this tax is to raise funds to administer the federal/state unemployment compensation program. The **SUTA** tax is also levied only on employers. The purpose of this tax is to raise funds to pay unemployment benefits.

The Social Security, FUTA, and SUTA taxes are calculated from the accumulated amounts found in the Taxable Earnings columns in the payroll register. The medicare tax is calculated from the Total Earnings column.

Objective 2.   Account for employer payroll taxes expense.

To journalize employer payroll taxes, debit the total of the employer Social Security, Medicare, FUTA, and SUTA taxes to a single account entitled Payroll Taxes Expense. The liabilities for the Social Security, Medicare, FUTA, and SUTA taxes payable normally are credited to separate accounts. The general format of this entry appears below:

Payroll Taxes Expense	xx	
Social Security Tax Payable		xx
Medicare Tax Payable		xx
FUTA Tax Payable		xx
SUTA Tax Payable		xx

Objective 3.   Describe employer reporting and payment responsibilities.

Employer payroll reporting and payment responsibilities fall in five areas:

1.   Federal income tax withholding and Social Security and Medicare taxes
2.   FUTA taxes
3.   SUTA taxes
4.   Employee Wage and Tax Statement (W-2)
5.   Summary of employee wages and taxes

The due date for federal income tax withholding and Social Security and Medicare taxes varies, depending on the amount of these taxes. Deposits are made using EFTPS or Form 8109. In addition, a Form 941 must be completed each quarter and filed with the IRS.

The federal unemployment taxes must be computed on a quarterly basis. In addition, Form 940 must be filed with the IRS at the end of the year.

Deposit rules and forms for state unemployment taxes vary among the states. Deposits usually are required on a quarterly basis.

Employers must furnish each employee with a Wage and Tax Statement (W-2) by January 31 of each year. Information needed to complete this form is contained in the employee earnings records. The employer also must file Form W-3 with the Social Security Administration by the last day of February. This form summarizes the employee earnings and tax information from Forms W-2.

Objective 4.   Describe and account for workers' compensation insurance.

Workers' compensation insurance provides insurance for employees who suffer a job-related illness or injury. The cost of the insurance depends on the number of employees, the riskiness of the job, and the company's accident history. The employer usually pays the premium at the beginning of the year, based on the estimated annual payroll, and makes an adjustment at the end of the year when the actual annual payroll is known.

REVIEW QUESTIONS

Instructions: Analyze each of the following carefully before writing your answer in the column at the right.

Question	Answer

LO 1   1. Name the four payroll taxes paid by the employer. ....

_____

_____

_____

_____

LO 1   2. The textbook uses a Social Security tax rate of 6.2% applied to maximum employee earnings of _____.......................................

_____

LO 1   3. The _____ is a key source of information for computing employer payroll taxes. ....

_____

LO 1   4. Individuals who own and run their own business are considered ____.

_____

LO 1   5. The law requires persons earning net self-employment income of $400 or more to pay a(n) _____...

_____

LO 1   6. The textbook uses a FUTA tax rate of 0.8% applied to maximum employee earnings of _____......................................

_____

LO 2   7. When journalizing the employer's payroll taxes, debit the total of the employer Social Security, Medicare, FUTA, and SUTA taxes to a single account entitled _____......................................

_____

LO 3   8. Name the three taxes that are associated with Form 941. ....

_____

_____

_____

LO 3   9. In addition to making quarterly deposits, employers are required to file an annual report of federal unemployment tax on Form _____.

_____

LO 3   10. By January 31 of each year, employers must furnish each employee with a(n) _____...

_____

LO 4   11. _____ provides insurance for employees who suffer a job-related illness or injury. ....

_____

EXERCISES AND PROBLEMS

Exercise 1 (LO 1) CALCULATION OF EMPLOYER PAYROLL TAXES

The Sylvania Bookstore pays a SUTA tax of 5.4% and a FUTA tax of 0.8%. The total taxable wages for unemployment compensation on a certain payday amount to $16,800. Compute the unemployment taxes payable to the state and federal government.

_____

_____

_____

_____

_____

_____

_____

_____

_____

_____

Exercise 2 (LO 2) CALCULATION OF PAYROLL TAXES AND PREPARATION OF JOURNAL ENTRIES

The totals line from Wong Drug Store's payroll register for the week ended December 31, 20— is shown on pages 122 and 123.

Payroll taxes are imposed as follows:

Social Security tax: 6.2%
Medicare tax: 1.45%
FUTA tax: 0.8%
SUTA tax: 5.4%

Required:

1. Prepare the journal entry for payment of this payroll on December 31, 20—.
2. Prepare the journal entry for the employer's payroll taxes for the period ended December 31, 20—.

Exercise 2 (Continued)

PAYROLL REGISTER

	NAME	EMPL. NO.	NO. ALLOW	MARIT. STATUS	EARNINGS							TAXABLE EARNINGS			
					REGULAR		OVERTIME		TOTAL		CUMULATIVE TOTAL		UNEMPLOY. COMP.		SOCIAL SECURITY	
1	Totals				4,200	00	500	00	4,700	00	203,700	00	300	00	3,600	00
2																
3																
4																
5																
6																
7																
8																
9																
10																

GENERAL JOURNAL   PAGE 1

	DATE		DESCRIPTION	POST. REF.	DEBIT	CREDIT	
1							1
2							2
3							3
4							4
5							5
6							6
7							7
8							8
9							9
10							10
11							11
12							12
13							13
14							14
15							15
16							16

Exercise 2 (Concluded)

FOR PERIOD ENDED DEC. 31

20--

FEDERAL INC. TAX		SOC. SEC. TAX		MEDICARE TAX		HEALTH INS.		CREDIT UNION		OTHER			TOTAL		NET PAY		CK. NO.	
420	00	223	20	68	15	80	00	200	00				991	35	3,708	65		1
																		2
																		3
																		4
																		5
																		6
																		7
																		8
																		9
																		10

Exercise 3 (LO1/2) TOTAL COST OF AN EMPLOYEE

Compute the total annual cost to an employer of employing a person whose gross salary is $45,000. (Assume a 5.4% state unemployment tax rate and a FUTA tax rate of 0.8%, both on the first $7,000 of earnings, an employer's Social Security tax rate of 6.2% on the first $87,000 of earnings and a Medicare tax rate of 1.45% on gross earnings.)

_____

_____

_____

_____

_____

_____

_____

_____

_____

Exercise 4 (LO 3) JOURNAL ENTRIES FOR PAYMENT OF PAYROLL TAXES

The general ledger of GNU Co. includes the following accounts and balances related to payroll as of October 15 of the current year.

Social Security Tax Payable	$3,100
Medicare Tax Payable	725
FUTA Tax Payable	160
SUTA Tax Payable	1,080
Employee Income Tax Payable	1,945

Required:

Journalize the Form 941 deposit of Social Security, Medicare and employee income taxes on October 15, 20--, and the deposit of the FUTA and SUTA taxes on October 31, 20--.

GENERAL JOURNAL   PAGE

	DATE	DESCRIPTION	POST. REF.	DEBIT	CREDIT	
1						1
2						2
3						3
4						4
5						5
6						6
7						7
8						8
9						9
10						10
11						11
12						12
13						13
14						14
15						15
16						16

Exercise 5 (LO 4) WORKERS' COMPENSATION INSURANCE AND ADJUSTMENT

Curtis Company paid a premium of $360 for workers' compensation insurance based on the estimated payroll as of the beginning of the year. Based on actual payroll as of the end of the year, the actual premium is $397. Prepare the adjusting entry to reflect the underpayment of the insurance premium.

GENERAL JOURNAL

PAGE 1

	DATE		DESCRIPTION	POST. REF.	DEBIT	CREDIT	
1							1
2							2
3							3
4							4
5							5
6							6
7							7
8							8
9							9
10							10
11							11
12							12
13							13

Problem 6 (LO 1/2) CALCULATING PAYROLL TAXES EXPENSE AND PREPARING JOURNAL ENTRY

A partial payroll register for the pay period ended August 31, 20— is provided on the following page for the Astroscope Company.

Required:

1. Compute the total earnings subject to federal and state unemployment taxes and the Social Security tax by completing the Taxable Earnings columns of the payroll register.

2. Assume the company is in a state with an unemployment tax rate of 5.4% and a FUTA tax rate of 0.8%, both on the first $7,000 of earnings. The Social Security tax rate is 6.2% on the first $87,000 of earnings, and Medicare tax rate is 1.45% on gross earnings. Compute the state and federal unemployment taxes and the Social Security and Medicare taxes on the lines provided on page 126.

3. Prepare the entry for the employer's payroll taxes in the general journal provided on page 127.

Problem 6 (Continued)

PAYROLL REGISTER

	NAME	NO. ALLOW.	MARIT. STATUS	EARNINGS						TAXABLE EARNINGS			
				REGULAR		OVERTIME		TOTAL		CUMULATIVE TOTAL		UNEMPLOY. COMP.	SOCIAL SECURITY
1	Coolie, Betty							350	00	7,150	00		
2	Covar, Mike							200	00	6,800	00		
3	Hagen, Frank							375	00	6,200	00		
4	Gutierrez, Bob							1,540	00	47,300	00		
5	Moten, Alice							1,500	00	50,500	00		
6	Rice, Darlene							3,300	00	89,900	00		
7													

Problem 6 (Concluded)

GENERAL JOURNAL

PAGE 1

	DATE		DESCRIPTION	POST. REF.	DEBIT	CREDIT	
1							1
2							2
3							3
4							4
5							5
6							6
7							7
8							8
9							9
10							10
11							11
12							12
13							13
14							14
15							15
16							16
17							17

Problem 7 (LO 2/3) JOURNALIZING AND POSTING PAYROLL ENTRIES

The Rock Creek Company has five employees. All are paid on a monthly basis. The fiscal year of the business is March 1 to February 28. Payroll taxes are imposed as follows:

Social Security tax to be withheld from employees' wages and imposed on the employer, 6.2% each on the first $87,000 of earnings.

Medicare tax to be withheld from employees' wages and imposed on the employer, 1.45% each on gross earnings.

SUTA tax imposed on the employer, 5.4% on the first $7,000 of earnings.

FUTA tax imposed on the employer, 0.8% on the first $7,000 of earnings.

Problem 7 (Continued)

The accounts kept by the Rock Creek Company include the following:

Account Number	Title	Balance on March 1
101	Cash	$45,800.00
211	Employee Income Tax Payable	1,125.00
212	Social Security Tax Payable	1,580.00
213	Medicare Tax Payable	370.00
218	Savings Bond Deductions Payable	400.00
221	FUTA Tax Payable	175.00
222	SUTA Tax Payable	890.00
511	Wages and Salaries Expense	-0-
530	Payroll Taxes Expense	-0-

Following is a narrative of selected transactions relating to payrolls and payroll taxes that occurred during the months of March and April.

March 15	Paid $3,075.00 covering the following February taxes:			
	Employee income tax withheld			$1,125.00
	Social Security tax			1,580.00
	Medicare tax			370.00
	Total			$3,075.00
31	March payroll:			
	Total wages and salaries expense			$13,000.00
	Less amounts withheld:			
	Employee income tax		$ 1,230.00	
	Social Security tax		806.00	
	Medicare tax		188.50	
	Savings bonds deductions payable		400.00	2,624.50
	Net amount paid			$10,375.50
31	Purchased savings bonds for employees, $800.00			
31	Data for completing employer's payroll taxes expense for March:			
	Social Security taxable wages			$13,000.00
	Unemployment taxable wages			4,000.00
April 15	Paid $3,219.00 covering the following March taxes:			
	Employee income tax payable			$ 1,230.00
	Social Security tax			1,612.00
	Medicare tax			377.00
30	Paid SUTA tax for the quarter, $1,106.00			
30	Paid FUTA tax, $207.00			

Problem 7 (Continued)

Required:

1. Using a general journal, journalize the preceding transactions.
2. Open T accounts for the payroll expense and liabilities. Enter the beginning balances and post the transactions recorded in the journal.

GENERAL JOURNAL

PAGE

	DATE	DESCRIPTION	POST. REF.	DEBIT	CREDIT	
1						1
2						2
3						3
4						4
5						5
6						6
7						7
8						8
9						9
10						10
11						11
12						12
13						13
14						14
15						15
16						16
17						17
18						18
19						19
20						20
21						21
22						22
23						23
24						24
25						25
26						26
27						27
28						28
29						29

Problem 7 (Continued)

Cash 101	Employ. Inc. Tax Pay. 211

Social Security Tax Payable 212	Medicare Tax Payable 213

Savings Bond Deductions Payable 218	FUTA Tax Payable 221

Problem 7 (Concluded)

SUTA Tax Payable	222		Wages and Salaries Expense	511

Payroll Taxes Expense	530

Problem 8 (LO 4) WORKERS' COMPENSATION INSURANCE AND ADJUSTMENT

Jackson Manufacturing estimated its total payroll for the coming year to be $630,000. The workers' compensation insurance premium rate is 0.35%.

Required:

1. Calculate the estimated workers' compensation insurance premium and prepare the journal entry for the payment as of January 2, 20—.

2. Assume Jackson Manufacturing's actual payroll for the year is $658,000. Calculate the total insurance premium owed. Prepare a journal entry as of December 31, 20—, to record the adjustment for the underpayment. The actual payment of the additional insurance premium will take place in January of the next year.

3. Assume, instead, that Jackson Manufacturing's actual payroll for the year is $607,000. Prepare a journal entry as of December 31, 20—, for the total amount that should be refunded. The refund will not be received until the next year.

GENERAL JOURNAL

PAGE 1

	DATE	DESCRIPTION	POST. REF.	DEBIT	CREDIT	
1						1
2						2
3						3
4						4
5						5
6						6
7						7
8						8
9						9
10						10
11						11
12						12
13						13
14						14
15						15
16						16
17						17
18						18
19						19

CHAPTER 10
ACCOUNTING FOR A PROFESSIONAL SERVICE BUSINESS: THE COMBINATION JOURNAL

LEARNING OBJECTIVES

The cash basis and modified cash basis are explained in Chapter 10 and then applied in the use of the combination journal. The combination journal is used for journalizing all transactions for a professional service business. Posting from a combination journal to the general ledger also is illustrated. Previously introduced, the work sheet and financial statements are also prepared following the transactions.

Objective 1.   Explain the cash, modified cash, and accrual bases of accounting.

The **accrual basis** of accounting recognizes revenues when earned, regardless of when cash is received. Likewise, expenses are recognized when incurred, regardless of when they are actually paid. The **cash basis** is used by some small businesses and by individuals for income tax purposes. With the cash basis, no revenue or expenses are recognized until cash is actually received or paid.

The **modified cash basis** is a combination of the accrual and cash methods. Revenues and most expenses are recorded only when cash is received or paid (like the cash basis). However, when cash is paid for assets with useful lives greater than one accounting period, exceptions are made. Cash payments like these are recorded as assets, and adjustments are made each period as under the accrual basis. Figure 10-2 in the text compares these methods in different types of transactions.

Objective 2.   Describe special records for a professional service business using the modified cash basis.

The modified cash basis is often used by small professional service businesses such as accounting, law, dentistry, medicine, and engineering. Since, under the modified cash basis, no adjusting entries are made for accrued wages expense and revenues from services performed on account are not recorded until cash is received, other records must be maintained. Two records commonly used are an appointment record and a client or patient ledger record.

Objective 3.   Describe and use a combination journal to record transactions of a professional service business.

The combination journal saves time, space, and energy in recording transactions (in comparison to the general journal). It also reduces the possibility of error since totals, rather than numerous individual entries, are posted. This is done by providing special columns for accounts frequently used. For example, the debits and credits to the cash account are posted only once—at the end of the month. Infrequently used accounts are entered in the General Debit column or the General Credit column. The Description column of a combination journal is used to enter account titles for the General Debit and General Credit columns, to identify specific creditors, to identify adjusting and closing entries, and to identify amounts forwarded from the previous page.

At the end of the accounting period, the sum of the debit columns should be compared with the sum of the credit columns to verify that they are equal. This is called proving the combination journal.

Objective 4.   Post from the combination journal to the general ledger.

Accounts that have been debited or credited in the general columns are posted individually from the combination journal. "CJ" and the page number are entered into the Posting Reference column of the general ledger account. Because individual items are posted, the totals of these columns are not posted, and check marks in parentheses are placed under the column totals.

Special columns are totaled and posted at the end of the accounting period. The account number is written in parentheses under the special column to show that the total has been posted.

The **cash balance** can be computed at any time during the month. The beginning balance (of the cash account) is added to the Cash debits (to date); the Cash credits (to date) are subtracted.

Objective 5. Prepare a work sheet, financial statements, and adjusting and closing entries for a professional service business.

When the combination journal has been posted to the general ledger, the end-of-period work sheet and financial statements are prepared in the same way as described in Chapters 5 and 6. By using the Description and General Debit and Credit columns, adjusting and closing entries are made in the combination journal in the same manner demonstrated for the general journal in Chapter 6.

REVIEW QUESTIONS

Instructions: Analyze each of the following items carefully before writing your answer in the column at the right.

	Question	**Answer**

LO 1 1. In the _____ basis of accounting, revenues are recorded when earned and expenses are recorded when incurred, regardless of when cash is received or paid. .... _____

LO 1 2. In the _____ basis of accounting, revenues are recorded only when cash is received and expenses are recorded only when cash is paid. ... _____

LO 1 3. The _____ basis of accounting uses the cash basis for revenues and most expenses. .... _____

LO 1 4. Many small professional _____ businesses use the modified cash basis of accounting. .... _____

LO 3 5. Time and space are saved when a journal contains _____ columns for cash debits and cash credits, rather than posting each transaction separately. .... _____

LO 3 6. When accounts are used infrequently, the _____ column and the _____ column are used for individual postings. .... _____

LO 3 7. A journal with special columns and general columns is called a(n) _____ journal. .... _____

LO 3 8. The _____ column is used to enter account titles, specific creditors and customers; and to identify adjusting and closing entries or amounts forwarded from the previous page. .... _____

LO 3 9. At the end of the month, all columns of the combination journal are _____, and the sums of the Debit columns are compared with the sums of the Credit columns. .... _____

LO 3 10. Totaling and ruling the columns and comparing totals is the process of _____ the combination journal. .... _____

LO 4 11. When posting from the combination journal, the letters " _____ are used. .... _____

LO 4 12. The cash balance at any time during the month is found by adding _____ to the beginning balance and subtracting _____ to date. _____

EXERCISES AND PROBLEMS

Exercise 1 (LO 1) CASH BASIS OF ACCOUNTING

In the space provided, indicate which account is debited and which account is credited, using the **cash basis** of accounting. If no entry is made, write "NO ENTRY."

1. Paid rent, $500.

_____

_____

2. Purchased typewriter (office equipment) for $300.

_____

_____

3. Revenue for week: $300 cash, $200 on account.

_____

_____

4. Purchased FAX machine (office equipment) for $400, on account.

_____

_____

5. Made payment on FAX machine, $100.

_____

_____

Exercise 2 (LO 1) MODIFIED CASH BASIS OF ACCOUNTING

In the space provided, indicate which account is debited and which account is credited, using the **modified cash basis** of accounting. If no entry is made, write "NO ENTRY."

1. Paid electricity bill, $50.

_____

_____

2. Purchased office equipment for $500, on account.

_____

_____

3. Revenue for week: $500 cash, $200 on account.

_____

_____

4. Wages earned but not paid, $500.

_____

_____

5. Made payment on office equipment previously purchased, $25.

_____

_____

Exercise 3 (LO 1) ACCRUAL BASIS OF ACCOUNTING

In the space provided, indicate which account is debited and which account is credited, using the **accrual basis** of accounting. If no entry is made, write "NO ENTRY."

1. Purchased supplies (prepaid asset), $500, on account.

_____

_____

2. Revenue for week: $400 cash, $250 on account.

_____

_____

3. Wages earned but not paid, $250.

_____

_____

Exercise 3 (Concluded)

4. Made payment on account, $50, for supplies previously purchased.

_____

_____

5. Depreciation on long-term assets, $300.

_____

_____

Exercise 4 (LO 3) SPECIAL COLUMNS FOR A COMBINATION JOURNAL

Ray Elkton is opening a delivery service. He owns a used van and will use it for deliveries. He has a part-time worker who is paid once a week. He receives delivery fees every three or four days and runs ads in the newspaper daily. Recommend to him which accounts should have **special columns** in a combination journal and give him three reasons why he should use a combination journal instead of a general journal.

Special Columns: _____

_____

Reasons:

1. _____

2. _____

3. _____

Problem 5 (LO 1) CASH, MODIFIED CASH, AND ACCRUAL BASES

Mark Mosley has his own consulting business. Listed below are selected transactions from the month of April:

April   1   Paid office rent, $500.

          2   Purchased office supplies, $250.

          3   Purchased office equipment on account, $1,000.

          4   Earned consulting fees: $400 cash, $150 on account.

          5   Paid telephone bill, $48.

          6   Purchased one-year insurance policy, $200.

          7   Paid $100 on account (for office equipment previously purchased).

          8   Received $150 on account from a customer (previously owed).

          9   Depreciation on office equipment for month, $50.

Required:

Record the transactions in the space provided, using:

1. the cash basis

2. the modified cash basis

3. the accrual basis

Problem 5 (Continued)

1. Cash Basis

GENERAL JOURNAL

PAGE

	DATE		DESCRIPTION	POST. REF.	DEBIT	CREDIT	
1							1
2							2
3							3
4							4
5							5
6							6
7							7
8							8
9							9
10							10
11							11
12							12
13							13
14							14
15							15
16							16
17							17
18							18
19							19
20							20
21							21
22							22
23							23
24							24
25							25
26							26
27							27
28							28
29							29
30							30

Problem 5 (Continued)

2. Modified Cash Basis

GENERAL JOURNAL   PAGE _____

	DATE		DESCRIPTION	POST. REF.	DEBIT	CREDIT	
1							1
2							2
3							3
4							4
5							5
6							6
7							7
8							8
9							9
10							10
11							11
12							12
13							13
14							14
15							15
16							16
17							17
18							18
19							19
20							20
21							21
22							22
23							23
24							24
25							25
26							26
27							27
28							28
29							29
30							30

Problem 5 (Concluded)

3. Accrual Basis

GENERAL JOURNAL

PAGE

	DATE		DESCRIPTION	POST. REF.	DEBIT	CREDIT	
1							1
2							2
3							3
4							4
5							5
6							6
7							7
8							8
9							9
10							10
11							11
12							12
13							13
14							14
15							15
16							16
17							17
18							18
19							19
20							20
21							21
22							22
23							23
24							24
25							25
26							26
27							27
28							28
29							29
30							30

Problem 6 (LO 3) JOURNAL ENTRIES USING A COMBINATION JOURNAL

Marilyn Davis is the owner of Davis Interior Designing that offers advice to clients wishing to decorate their homes. Listed below are representative transactions for the month of February:

Feb.	1	Issued a check for $500 to Pedro Rodriguez for the February office rent.
	3	Received $300 for services rendered to Linda Johnson.
	5	Issued a check for $800 to Maxwell's Office Supply to purchase office equipment.
	10	Invested $5,000 additional cash in the business.
	28	Issued a check for $400 to Homer Utilities in payment of electric and water bill.
	28	Issued a check for $200 to Buck's Furniture for payment on office furniture previously purchased.

Required:

1. Davis uses the **modified cash basis** of accounting. Enter the above transactions in the combination journal shown on pages 142–143.

2. Total and prove the combination journal.

Problem 6 (Continued)

COMBINATION

	DATE		CASH			DESCRIPTION	POST. REF.	
			DEBIT	CREDIT				
1								1
2								2
3								3
4								4
5								5
6								6
7								7
8								8
9								9
10								10
11								11
12								12
13								13
14								14

Proving the Combination Journal:

_____

_____

_____

_____

_____

_____

_____

_____

_____

_____

Problem 6 (Concluded)

JOURNAL   PAGE

	GENERAL			CLIENT FEES CREDIT	RENT EXPENSE DEBIT	UTILITIES EXPENSE DEBIT	
	DEBIT		CREDIT				
1							1
2							2
3							3
4							4
5							5
6							6
7							7
8							8
9							9
10							10
11							11
12							12
13							13
14							14

Problem 7 (LO3/4/5) JOURNALIZING AND POSTING TRANSACTIONS AND PREPARING A TRIAL BALANCE

Jolene Knight operates a cartographer's map service, Knight Maps. During the month of May, she entered the following transactions:

May	1	Issued a check for $400 to purchase new surveying equipment.
	3	Received a check for $900 from Diane Branam for surveying her property. Earned $1,500 on account from Troy Laakman.
	4	Issued a check for $600 to CFC Rental to pay May office rent.
	6	Purchased office supplies from Bynum Office Supply on account, $250.
	10	Received a check for $3,500 from B. Sims, a real estate developer, for surveying a new subdivision.
	12	Issued a check for $300 to Oscar Miller, a part-time secretary.
	15	Issued a check for $85 to Winona's Service Station for gas and oil for the business truck.
	16	Issued a check for $200 to Bynum Office Supply in payment on account.
	18	Issued a check for $150 to George Wilson, a part-time employee.
	20	Issued a check for $200 to Winona's Service Station for work done on a company truck.
	22	Issued a check for $100 to the American Cancer Society.
	25	Received a check for $1,500 from Troy Laakman for surveying work previously performed.
	30	Issued a check for $500 as a personal withdrawal from the business.
	31	Issued a check for $300 to Oscar Miller, a part-time secretary.

Required:
1. Using the **modified cash basis** of accounting, enter the above transactions in the combination journal provided on pages 144–145.
2. Prove the combination journal.
3. Post the entries from the combination journal to the ledger accounts provided on pages 145–148.
4. Prepare a trial balance for Knight Maps as of May 31, 20—, to confirm accuracy of the debits and credits.

Problem 7 (Continued)

COMBINATION

	DATE		CASH								DESCRIPTION	POST. REF.	
			DEBIT				CREDIT						
1													1
2													2
3													3
4													4
5													5
6													6
7													7
8													8
9													9
10													10
11													11
12													12
13													13
14													14
15													15
16													16
17													17
18													18
19													19
20													20

Proving the Combination Journal:

_____

_____

_____

_____

_____

_____

_____

_____

Problem 7 (Continued)

JOURNAL

PAGE

	GENERAL		CLIENT FEES CREDIT	WAGES EXPENSE DEBIT	TRUCK EXPENSE DEBIT	
	DEBIT	CREDIT				
1						1
2						2
3						3
4						4
5						5
6						6
7						7
8						8
9						9
10						10
11						11
12						12
13						13
14						14
15						15
16						16
17						17
18						18
19						19
20						20

GENERAL LEDGER

ACCOUNT Cash

ACCOUNT NO. 101

DATE	ITEM	POST. REF.	DEBIT	CREDIT	BALANCE	
					DEBIT	CREDIT
20— May 1	Balance	√			1 2 0 0 00	

Problem 7 (Continued)

ACCOUNT   Office Supplies   ACCOUNT NO.   142

DATE		ITEM	POST. REF.	DEBIT	CREDIT	BALANCE	
						DEBIT	CREDIT
20— May	1	Balance	√			1 0 0 00	

ACCOUNT   Surveying Equipment   ACCOUNT NO.   181

DATE		ITEM	POST. REF.	DEBIT	CREDIT	BALANCE	
						DEBIT	CREDIT
20— May	1	Balance	√			13 0 0 0 00	

ACCOUNT   Accumulated Depreciation—Surveying Equipment   ACCOUNT NO.   181.1

DATE		ITEM	POST. REF.	DEBIT	CREDIT	BALANCE	
						DEBIT	CREDIT

ACCOUNT   Truck   ACCOUNT NO.   185

DATE		ITEM	POST. REF.	DEBIT	CREDIT	BALANCE	
						DEBIT	CREDIT
20— May	1	Balance	√			12 0 0 0 00	

ACCOUNT   Accumulated Depreciation—Truck   ACCOUNT NO.   185.1

DATE		ITEM	POST. REF.	DEBIT	CREDIT	BALANCE	
						DEBIT	CREDIT

ACCOUNT   Notes Payable   ACCOUNT NO.   201

DATE		ITEM	POST. REF.	DEBIT	CREDIT	BALANCE	
						DEBIT	CREDIT
20— May	1	Balance	√				10 0 0 0 00

Name _____

Problem 7 (Continued)

ACCOUNT Accounts Payable   ACCOUNT NO. 202

DATE	ITEM	POST. REF.	DEBIT	CREDIT	BALANCE DEBIT	BALANCE CREDIT
20— May 1	Balance	√				2 0 0 00

ACCOUNT Jolene Knight, Capital   ACCOUNT NO. 311

DATE	ITEM	POST. REF.	DEBIT	CREDIT	BALANCE DEBIT	BALANCE CREDIT
20— May 1	Balance	√				12 7 0 0 00

ACCOUNT Jolene Knight, Drawing   ACCOUNT NO. 312

DATE	ITEM	POST. REF.	DEBIT	CREDIT	BALANCE DEBIT	BALANCE CREDIT
20— May 1	Balance	√			1 0 0 0 00	

ACCOUNT Client Fees   ACCOUNT NO. 401

DATE	ITEM	POST. REF.	DEBIT	CREDIT	BALANCE DEBIT	BALANCE CREDIT
20— May 1	Balance	√				12 0 0 0 00

ACCOUNT Wages Expense   ACCOUNT NO. 511

DATE	ITEM	POST. REF.	DEBIT	CREDIT	BALANCE DEBIT	BALANCE CREDIT
20— May 1	Balance	√			4 0 0 0 00	

Problem 7 (Continued)

ACCOUNT   Rent Expense   ACCOUNT NO.   521

DATE		ITEM	POST. REF.	DEBIT	CREDIT	BALANCE	
						DEBIT	CREDIT
20—							
May	3	Balance	√			2 4 0 0 00	

ACCOUNT   Truck Expense   ACCOUNT NO.   526

DATE		ITEM	POST. REF.	DEBIT	CREDIT	BALANCE	
						DEBIT	CREDIT
20—							
May	1	Balance	√			8 0 0 00	

ACCOUNT   Charitable Contributions Expense   ACCOUNT NO.   534

DATE		ITEM	POST. REF.	DEBIT	CREDIT	BALANCE	
						DEBIT	CREDIT
20—							
May	1	Balance	√			4 0 0 00	

ACCOUNT   Depreciation Expense—Surveying Equipment   ACCOUNT NO.   541

DATE		ITEM	POST. REF.	DEBIT	CREDIT	BALANCE	
						DEBIT	CREDIT

ACCOUNT   Depreciation Expense—Truck   ACCOUNT NO.   542

DATE		ITEM	POST. REF.	DEBIT	CREDIT	BALANCE	
						DEBIT	CREDIT

Problem 7 (Concluded)

ACCOUNT	ACCT. NO.	DEBIT BALANCE	CREDIT BALANCE

Problem 8 (LO 5) PREPARING A WORK SHEET, FINANCIAL STATEMENTS, ADJUSTING AND CLOSING ENTRIES

The work sheet for Charlotte Cruz, a financial planner, is shown on pages 150–151. The Trial Balance columns have been completed. There were no additional investments by the owner.
Adjustments are as follows:

(a) Prepaid insurance expired, $200.

(b) Unused office supplies on hand, $228.

(c) Depreciation expense—office equipment, $125.

Required:

1. Finish the work sheet.

2. Prepare the income statement, statement of owner's equity, and balance sheet.

3. Record the adjusting entries and closing entries in the combination journal on pages 154–155.

Problem 8 (Continued)

CRUZ FINANCIAL

WORK

FOR MONTH

	ACCOUNT TITLE	TRIAL BALANCE		ADJUSTMENTS	
		DEBIT	CREDIT	DEBIT	CREDIT
1	Cash	3 0 8 2 00			
2	Office Supplies	6 2 8 00			
3	Prepaid Insurance	3 5 0 00			
4	Office Equipment	1 8 0 0 00			
5	Accum. Depr.—Office Equipment		2 5 0 00		
6	Accounts Payable		9 0 0 00		
7	Charlotte Cruz, Capital		3 0 0 0 00		
8	Charlotte Cruz, Drawing	1 0 0 00			
9	Planning Fees		3 0 2 6 00		
10	Wages Expense	8 0 0 00			
11	Rent Expense	3 0 0 00			
12	Office Supplies Expense				
13	Telephone Expense	5 2 00			
14	Electricity Expense	3 8 00			
15	Insurance Expense				
16	Depreciation Exp.—Office Equip				
17	Miscellaneous Expense	2 6 00			
18	Net Income	7 1 7 6 00	7 1 7 6 00		
19					
20					
21					
22					
23					
24					
25					
26					
27					
28					
29					
30					
31					

Problem 8 (Continued)

PLANNING

SHEET

ENDED DECEMBER 31, 20--

ADJUSTED TRIAL BALANCE		INCOME STATEMENT		BALANCE SHEET		
DEBIT	CREDIT	DEBIT	CREDIT	DEBIT	CREDIT	
						1
						2
						3
						4
						5
						6
						7
						8
						9
						10
						11
						12
						13
						14
						15
						16
						17
						18
						19
						20
						21
						22
						23
						24
						25
						26
						27
						28
						29
						30
						31

Problem 8 (Continued)

Problem 8 (Continued)

Problem 8 (Continued)

COMBINATION

	DATE		CASH			DESCRIPTION	POST. REF.	
			DEBIT	CREDIT				
1								1
2								2
3								3
4								4
5								5
6								6
7								7
8								8
9								9
10								10
11								11
12								12
13								13
14								14
15								15
16								16
17								17
18								18
19								19
20								20
21								21
22								22
23								23
24								24
25								25
26								26
27								27
28								28

Problem 8 (Concluded)

JOURNAL   PAGE ____

| | GENERAL | | PLANNING FEES CREDIT | WAGES EXPENSE DEBIT | MISC. EXPENSE DEBIT | |
	DEBIT	CREDIT				
1						1
2						2
3						3
4						4
5						5
6						6
7						7
8						8
9						9
10						10
11						11
12						12
13						13
14						14
15						15
16						16
17						17
18						18
19						19
20						20
21						21
22						22
23						23
24						24
25						25
26						26
27						27
28						28

Notes

End Page of Study Guide

End Page of Working Papers

Notes

Problem 8 (Continued)

PLANNING

SHEET

ENDED DECEMBER 31, 20--

ADJUSTED TRIAL BALANCE		INCOME STATEMENT		BALANCE SHEET		
DEBIT	CREDIT	DEBIT	CREDIT	DEBIT	CREDIT	
						1
						2
						3
						4
						5
						6
						7
						8
						9
						10
						11
						12
						13
						14
						15
						16
						17
						18
						19
						20
						21
						22
						23
						24
						25
						26
						27
						28
						29
						30
						31

Problem 8 (Continued)

Name _____

Problem 8 (Continued)

Problem 8 (Continued)

COMBINATION

	DATE		CASH				DESCRIPTION	POST. REF.	
			DEBIT		CREDIT				
1									1
2									2
3									3
4									4
5									5
6									6
7									7
8									8
9									9
10									10
11									11
12									12
13									13
14									14
15									15
16									16
17									17
18									18
19									19
20									20
21									21
22									22
23									23
24									24
25									25
26									26
27									27
28									28

Problem 8 (Concluded)

JOURNAL   PAGE

	GENERAL		PLANNING FEES CREDIT	WAGES EXPENSE DEBIT	MISC. EXPENSE DEBIT	
	DEBIT	CREDIT				
1						1
2						2
3						3
4						4
5						5
6						6
7						7
8						8
9						9
10						10
11						11
12						12
13						13
14						14
15						15
16						16
17						17
18						18
19						19
20						20
21						21
22						22
23						23
24						24
25						25
26						26
27						27
28						28

Notes

End Page of Study Guide

Exercise 1-1A

1. _____ Owners

2. _____ Managers

3. _____ Creditors

4. _____ Governmental
   agencies

a. whether the firm can pay its bills on time

b. detailed, up-to-date information to measure business
   performance (and plan for future operations)

c. to determine taxes to be paid and whether other
   regulations are met.

d. the firm's current financial condition

Exercise 1-2A

Order	Accounting Process	Definition
_____	Recording	_____
		_____
		_____
_____	Summarizing	_____
		_____
		_____
_____	Reporting	_____
		_____
		_____
_____	Analyzing	_____
		_____
		_____
_____	Interpreting	_____
		_____
		_____
_____	Classifying	_____
		_____
		_____

Exercise 1-1B

<u>Users</u>	<u>Information</u>
Owners (present and future):	_____
	_____
	_____
Managers:	_____
	_____
	_____
Creditors (present and future):	_____
	_____
	_____
Government agencies:	_____
	_____
	_____

Exercise 1-2B

<u>Letter</u>	<u>Accounting Process</u>
_____	Analyzing
_____	Recording
_____	Classifying
_____	Summarizing
_____	Reporting
_____	Interpreting

<u>Definition</u>

a. telling the results

b. looking at events that have taken place and thinking about how they affect the business

c. deciding the importance of the various reports

d. bringing together information to explain a result

e. sorting and grouping like items together

f. entering financial information into the accounting system

Exercise 2-1A

Item	Account	Classification
Money in bank	Cash	_____
Office supplies	Supplies	_____
Money owed	Accounts Payable	_____
Office chairs	Office Furniture	_____
Net worth of owner	John Smith, Capital	_____
Money withdrawn by owner	John Smith, Drawing	_____
Money owed us by customers	Accounts Receivable	_____

Exercise 2-2A

Assets	=	Liabilities	+	Owner's Equity
_____	=	$24,000	+	$10,000
$25,000	=	$18,000	+	_____
$40,000	=	_____	+	$15,000

Exercise 2-3A

	Assets	=	Liabilities	+	Owner's Equity
(a)	_____		_____		_____
Bal.	_____		_____		_____
(b)	_____		_____		_____
Bal.	_____		_____		_____
(c)	_____		_____		_____
	_____		_____		_____
Bal.	_____		_____		_____
(d)	_____		_____		_____
Bal.	_____		_____		_____

Exercise 2-4A

	Assets	=	Liabilities	+	Capital	–	Drawing	+	Revenues	–	Expenses	Description
					Owner's Equity							
Bal.												
(e)												
Bal.												
(f)												
Bal.												
(g)												
Bal.												
(h)												
Bal.												
(i)												
Bal.												
(j)												
Bal.												
(k)												
Bal.												

Exercise 2-5A

Account	Classification	Financial Statement
Cash		
Rent Expense		
Accounts Payable		
Service Fees		
Supplies		
Wages Expense		
Ramon Martinez, Drawing		
Ramon Martinez, Capital		
Prepaid Insurance		
Accounts Receivable		

Exercise 2-6A

Exercise 2-7A

Problem 2-8A

	Assets	=	Liabilities	+	Owner's Equity
1.					
2.					
3.					

Problem 2-9A: See page WP-7

Problem 2-10A

Problem 2-9A

	Assets				=	Liabilities	+	Owner's Equity				
	Cash	+ Accounts Receivable	+ Office Supplies	+ Prepaid Insurance	=	Accounts Payable	+ J. Pembroke, Capital	− J Pembroke, Drawing	+ Revenues	− Expenses	Description
(a)	18,000						18,000				
Bal.	18,000						18,000				
(b)	(2,000)		4,600	2,600		26,000					
Bal.	16,000										
(c)	(1,200)			1,200							
Bal.	14,800	2,000	4,600	1,200		26,000	18,000				
(d)	1,300	2,000							3,300		Svc fees
Bal.	16,100	2,000	4,600	1,200		26,000	18,000		3,300		
(e)	(2,300)					(2,300)					
Bal.	13,800					300				750	
(f)	(750)									750	Rent exp
Bal.	13,050	2,000	4,600	1,200		300	18,000		3,300	750	
(g)	(1,01)										
Bal.	12,950										

$$20,750 = 20,750$$

Problem 2-11A

Problem 2-12A

Mastery Problem

1.

	Assets						=	Liabilities +	Owner's Equity					
		Items Owned						Amts. Owed	Owner's Investment				Earnings	
Cash	+	Accts. Rec.	+	Sup- plies	+	Prepaid Ins.	+	Tools	+	Van	=	Accts. Payable	+	L. Vozniak, Capital	−	L. Vozniak, Drawing	+	Rev.	−	Exp.	Description
(a)																				
Bal.																				
(b)																				
Bal.																				
(c)																				
Bal.																				
(d)																				
Bal.																				
(e)																				
Bal.																				
(f)																				
Bal.																				
(g)																				
Bal.																				
(h)																				
Bal.																				
(i)																				
Bal.																				
(j)																				
Bal.																				

Continued on next page

Mastery Problem (Continued)

	Assets					=	Liabilities	+	Owner's Equity				
	Items Owned						Amts. Owed		Owner's Investment			Earnings		
Cash	Accts. Rec.	Sup- plies	Prepaid Ins.	Tools	Van	=	Accts. Payable	+	L. Vozniak, Capital	L. Vozniak, Drawing	Rev.	Exp.	Description
+	+	+	+	+		=		+	+	−	+	−	
(k)													
Bal.													
(l)													
Bal.													
(m)													
Bal.													
(n)													
Bal.													
(o)													
Bal.													
(p)													
Bal.													

Mastery Problem (Continued)

3.

4.

Mastery Problem (Concluded)

5.

Challenge Problem

Cash from customers				
Cash paid for wages				
Cash paid for rent				
Cash paid for utilities				
Cash paid for insurance				
Cash paid for supplies				
Cash paid for telephone				
Total cash paid for operating items				
Difference between cash received from customers and				
cash paid for goods and services				

Exercise 3-1A

Cash
|

Exercise 3-2A

a.   The cash account is increased with a...   _____

b.   The owner's capital account is increased with a...   _____

c.   The delivery equipment account is increased with a ....   _____

d.   The cash account is decreased with a ....   _____

e.   The liability account Accounts Payable is increased with a ....   _____

f.   The revenue account Delivery Fees is increased with a..   _____

g.   The asset account Accounts Receivable is increased with a....................................   _____

h.   The rent expense account is increased with a...   _____

i.   The owner's drawing account is increased with a..   _____

Exercise 3-3A

1. & 2.

Cash   Jim Arnold, Capital
| |

Supplies   Utilities Expense
| |

Exercise 3-4A

Account	Debit or Credit
1. Cash	debit
2. Wages Expense	debit
3. Accounts Payable	credit
4. Owner's Drawing	debit
5. Supplies	debit
6. Owner's Capital	credit
7. Equipment	debit

Exercise 3-5A: See page WP-23

Exercise 3-6A

Cash

Exercise 3-5A

Assets		=	Liabilities		+	Owner's Equity	
Dr.	Cr.		Dr.	Cr.		Dr.	Cr.
+	−		−	+		−	+

Drawing
Dr.	Cr.
+	−

Expenses
Dr.	Cr.
+	−

Revenues
Dr.	Cr.
−	+

Exercise 3-7A

Assets			=	Liabilities			+	Owner's Equity		
Dr.	Cr.			Dr.	Cr.			Dr.	Cr.	
+	–			–	+			–	+	

Drawing

Dr.	Cr.
+	–

Expenses

Dr.	Cr.
+	–

Revenues

Dr.	Cr.
–	+

Exercise 3-8A

ACCOUNT	DEBIT BALANCE	CREDIT BALANCE

Exercise 3-9A

ACCOUNT	DEBIT BALANCE	CREDIT BALANCE

Exercise 3-10A

Exercise 3-11A

Exercise 3-12A

Problem 3-13A, 1. & 2

Assets			=	Liabilities		
Dr. +		Cr. −		Dr. −		Cr. +

Cash

Dr. +	Cr. −
a. 20,000	b. 7,000
d. 6,000	e. 3,000
i. 3,000	f. 900
o. 1,400	g. 200
	i. 120
	j. 600
	k. 1,200
	m. 160
	n. 1,000
	p. 2,800
30,200	15,980
a. 14,878	

A/R

Dr. +	Cr. −
h. 4,000	
o. 1,400	

A/P

Dr. −	Cr. +
e. 2,000	b. 5,000
	h. 2,000
	7,000
	2,000
Bal	5,000

Supplies

Dr. +	Cr. −
c. 900	
j. 3,000	
Bal	120

Prepaid Ins.

Dr. +	Cr. −
k. 1,200	

Equip.

Dr. +	Cr. −
b. 5,000	
n. 3,000	

W/T

b. 8,000	
g. 2,000	

Owner's Equity

Dr. −		Cr. +

H. Long, Capital

Dr. −	Cr. +
	a. 20,000

Drawing

Dr. +	Cr. −

H. Long, Drawing

Dr. +	Cr. −
p. 2,800	

Expenses

Dr. +	Cr. −

Rent

Dr. +	Cr. −
f. 900	

Wages

Telephone

g. 200	

Gas & Oil

m. 160	

Revenues

Dr. −	Cr. +

Sales Fees

Dr. −	Cr. +
	d. 6,000
	h. 4,000
	i. 3,000
	13,000

Problem 3-13A (Concluded)

3.

Harold Home Repair
Trial Balance
May 31, 2007

ACCOUNT	DEBIT BALANCE	CREDIT BALANCE
Cash	14820 00	
A/R	2400 00	
Supplies	120 00	
Prepaid Ins.	1200 00	
Equip	8000 00	
Van	7000 00	
Accts Pay		5000 00
H Long Capital		20000 00
H Long Drawing	2800 00	
Svc Fees		13200 00
Rent	900 00	
Wages	600 00	
Phone	200 00	
Gas	160 00	
Total	38200 00	38200 00

Problem 3-14A

1.

(a) Total revenue for the month .... _____

(b) Total expenses for the month .... _____

(c) Net income for the month .... _____

2.

(a) Harold Long's original investment in the business............. _____

    + The net income for the month ...._____

    − Owner's drawing ...._____

    = Ending owner's equity... _____

(b) End of month accounting equation:

Assets	=	Liabilities	+	Owner's Equity

Problem 3-15A

1.

Exercise 3-7B

Assets		=	Liabilities		+	Owner's Equity	
Dr. +	Cr. –		Dr. –	Cr. +		Dr. –	Cr. +

Drawing			Expenses			Revenues	
Dr. +	Cr. –		Dr. +	Cr. –		Dr. –	Cr. +

Exercise 3-8B

ACCOUNT	DEBIT BALANCE	CREDIT BALANCE

Mastery Problem
1 & 2.

Assets		=	Liabilities		+	Owner's Equity	
Dr. +	Cr. −		Dr. −	Cr. +		Dr. −	Cr. +

Drawing			Expenses			Revenues	
Dr. +	Cr. −		Dr. +	Cr. −		Dr. −	Cr. +

Mastery Problem (Continued)

3.

ACCOUNT	DEBIT BALANCE	CREDIT BALANCE

4.

	DEBIT BALANCE	CREDIT BALANCE

Mastery Problem (Concluded)

5.

6.

Challenge Problem

1.

Exercise 4-1A

1. _____*c*_____ Check stubs or check register

2. _____*d.*_____ Purchase invoice from suppliers (vendors)

3. _____*a.*_____ Sales tickets or invoices to customers

4. _____*b.*_____ Receipts or cash register tapes

a. A good or service has been sold.

b. Cash has been received by the business.

c. Cash has been paid by the business.

d. Goods or services have been purchased by the business.

Exercise 4-2A

Transaction	Debit	Credit
1. Invested cash in the business, $5,000.		
2. Paid office rent, $500.		
3. Purchased office supplies on account, $300.		
4. Received cash for services rendered (fees), $400.		
5. Paid cash on account, $50.		
6. Rendered services on account, $300.		
7. Received cash for an amount owed by a customer, $100.		

Exercise 4-3A

Exercise 4-3A (Concluded)

Exercise 4-4A

GENERAL JOURNAL

PAGE 1

	DATE		DESCRIPTION	POST. REF.	DEBIT	CREDIT	
1	2007 Jan	1	Cash		10 0 0 0 00		1
2			Jean Jones, Capital			10 0 0 0 00	2
3			Jones invested in company				3
4							4
5		2	Rent Expense		5 0 0 00		5
6			Cash			5 0 0 00	6
7			paid rent (Jan)				7
8							8
9		3	Office Equipment		15 0 0 00		9
10			Accts Payable			15 0 0 00	10
11			purchased office equip on acct.				11
12							12
13		5	Cash		7 5 0 00		13
14			Consulting fees			7 5 0 00	14
15			rec, cash for svcs.				15
16							16
17		8	Telephone Expenses		6 5 00		17
18			Cash			6 5 00	18
19			paid telephone bill for Jan.				19
20							20
21		10	Miscellaneous Expense		1 5 00		21
22			Cash			1 5 00	22
23			purchased subscription				23
24							24

Exercise 4-4A (Concluded)

GENERAL JOURNAL

	DATE		DESCRIPTION	POST. REF.	DEBIT	CREDIT	
1	2007 Jan	11	Office Supplies		30000		1
2			Accts Payable			30000	2
3			purchased office supplies on acct				3
4							4
5		15	Accts Payable		15000		5
6			Cash			15000	6
7			payment on acct.				7
8							8
9		18	Wage Expense		50000		9
10			Cash			50000	10
11			paid pt-time employee				11
12							12
13		21	Cash		35000		13
14			consulting fees			35000	14
15			for svcs rendered				15
16							16
17		25	utility Expense		8500		17
18			Cash			8500	18
19			paid utility bill				19
20							20
21		27	Jones Drawing		10000		21
22			Cash			10000	22
23			withdrew cash				23
24							24
25		29	Wages Expense		50000		25
26			Cash			50000	26
27			pd pt-time employee				27
28							28
29							29
30							30
31							31
32							32
33							33
34							34
35							35
36							36

Exercise 4-5A

GENERAL LEDGER

ACCOUNT _____ ACCOUNT NO. _____

DATE	ITEM	POST. REF.	DEBIT	CREDIT	BALANCE	
					DEBIT	CREDIT

ACCOUNT _____ ACCOUNT NO. _____

DATE	ITEM	POST. REF.	DEBIT	CREDIT	BALANCE	
					DEBIT	CREDIT

ACCOUNT _____ ACCOUNT NO. _____

DATE	ITEM	POST. REF.	DEBIT	CREDIT	BALANCE	
					DEBIT	CREDIT

Exercise 4-5A (Continued)

ACCOUNT _____   ACCOUNT NO. _____

DATE	ITEM	POST. REF.	DEBIT	CREDIT	BALANCE DEBIT	BALANCE CREDIT

ACCOUNT _____   ACCOUNT NO. _____

DATE	ITEM	POST. REF.	DEBIT	CREDIT	BALANCE DEBIT	BALANCE CREDIT

ACCOUNT _____   ACCOUNT NO. _____

DATE	ITEM	POST. REF.	DEBIT	CREDIT	BALANCE DEBIT	BALANCE CREDIT

ACCOUNT _____   ACCOUNT NO. _____

DATE	ITEM	POST. REF.	DEBIT	CREDIT	BALANCE DEBIT	BALANCE CREDIT

Exercise 4-5A (Continued)

ACCOUNT _____ ACCOUNT NO. _____

DATE	ITEM	POST. REF.	DEBIT	CREDIT	BALANCE	
					DEBIT	CREDIT

ACCOUNT _____ ACCOUNT NO. _____

DATE	ITEM	POST. REF.	DEBIT	CREDIT	BALANCE	
					DEBIT	CREDIT

ACCOUNT _____ ACCOUNT NO. _____

DATE	ITEM	POST. REF.	DEBIT	CREDIT	BALANCE	
					DEBIT	CREDIT

ACCOUNT _____ ACCOUNT NO. _____

DATE	ITEM	POST. REF.	DEBIT	CREDIT	BALANCE	
					DEBIT	CREDIT

ACCOUNT _____ ACCOUNT NO. _____

DATE	ITEM	POST. REF.	DEBIT	CREDIT	BALANCE	
					DEBIT	CREDIT

Exercise 4-5A (Concluded)

ACCOUNT	ACCT. NO.	DEBIT BALANCE	CREDIT BALANCE

Exercise 4-6A

Exercise 4-6A (Concluded)

Exercise 4-7A

Exercise 4-7A (Concluded)

Exercise 4-8A

GENERAL JOURNAL

PAGE

	DATE		DESCRIPTION	POST. REF.	DEBIT	CREDIT	
15	May	17	Office Equipment		4 0 0 00		15
16			Cash			4 0 0 00	16
17			Purchased copy paper				17
18							18
23		23	Cash	101	1 0 0 0 00		23
24			Service Fees	401		1 0 0 0 00	24
25			Received cash for services previously earned				25
26							26
27							27
28							28
29							29
30							30
31							31
32							32
33							33

Problem 4-9A
2. (For 1. & 3., see page WP-60)

GENERAL JOURNAL　　　　　　　　　PAGE　7

	DATE		DESCRIPTION	POST. REF.	DEBIT	CREDIT	
1							1
2							2
3							3
4							4
5							5
6							6
7							7
8							8
9							9
10							10
11							11
12							12
13							13
14							14
15							15
16							16
17							17
18							18
19							19
20							20
21							21
22							22
23							23
24							24
25							25
26							26
27							27
28							28
29							29
30							30
31							31
32							32
33							33
34							34

Problem 4-9A (Continued)

GENERAL JOURNAL   PAGE 8

	DATE		DESCRIPTION	POST. REF.	DEBIT	CREDIT	
1							1
2							2
3							3
4							4
5							5
6							6
7							7
8							8
9							9
10							10
11							11
12							12
13							13
14							14
15							15
16							16
17							17
18							18
19							19
20							20
21							21
22							22
23							23
24							24
25							25
26							26
27							27
28							28
29							29
30							30
31							31
32							32
33							33
34							34
35							35
36							36

Problem 4-9A (Continued)

GENERAL JOURNAL

	DATE		DESCRIPTION	POST. REF.	DEBIT	CREDIT	
1							1
2							2
3							3
4							4
5							5
6							6
7							7
8							8
9							9
10							10
11							11
12							12
13							13
14							14
15							15
16							16
17							17
18							18
19							19
20							20
21							21
22							22
23							23
24							24
25							25
26							26
27							27
28							28
29							29
30							30
31							31
32							32
33							33
34							34
35							35
36							36

Problem 4-9A (Continued)

1. & 3.

ACCOUNT Cash   ACCOUNT NO. 101

DATE	ITEM	POST. REF.	DEBIT	CREDIT	BALANCE	
					DEBIT	CREDIT

Problem 4-9A (Continued)

ACCOUNT Accounts Receivable   ACCOUNT NO. 122

DATE	ITEM	POST. REF.	DEBIT	CREDIT	BALANCE	
					DEBIT	CREDIT

ACCOUNT Office Supplies   ACCOUNT NO. 142

DATE	ITEM	POST. REF.	DEBIT	CREDIT	BALANCE	
					DEBIT	CREDIT

ACCOUNT Office Equipment   ACCOUNT NO. 181

DATE	ITEM	POST. REF.	DEBIT	CREDIT	BALANCE	
					DEBIT	CREDIT

ACCOUNT Delivery Truck   ACCOUNT NO. 185

DATE	ITEM	POST. REF.	DEBIT	CREDIT	BALANCE	
					DEBIT	CREDIT

Problem 4-9A (Continued)

ACCOUNT Accounts Payable   ACCOUNT NO. 202

DATE	ITEM	POST. REF.	DEBIT	CREDIT	BALANCE DEBIT	BALANCE CREDIT

ACCOUNT Jim Andrews, Capital   ACCOUNT NO. 311

DATE	ITEM	POST. REF.	DEBIT	CREDIT	BALANCE DEBIT	BALANCE CREDIT

ACCOUNT Jim Andrews, Drawing   ACCOUNT NO. 312

DATE	ITEM	POST. REF.	DEBIT	CREDIT	BALANCE DEBIT	BALANCE CREDIT

ACCOUNT Delivery Fees   ACCOUNT NO. 401

DATE	ITEM	POST. REF.	DEBIT	CREDIT	BALANCE DEBIT	BALANCE CREDIT

Problem 4-9A (Continued)

ACCOUNT Wages Expense   ACCOUNT NO. 511

DATE	ITEM	POST. REF.	DEBIT	CREDIT	BALANCE DEBIT	BALANCE CREDIT

ACCOUNT Advertising Expense   ACCOUNT NO. 512

DATE	ITEM	POST. REF.	DEBIT	CREDIT	BALANCE DEBIT	BALANCE CREDIT

ACCOUNT Rent Expense   ACCOUNT NO. 521

DATE	ITEM	POST. REF.	DEBIT	CREDIT	BALANCE DEBIT	BALANCE CREDIT

ACCOUNT Telephone Expense   ACCOUNT NO. 525

DATE	ITEM	POST. REF.	DEBIT	CREDIT	BALANCE DEBIT	BALANCE CREDIT

Problem 4-9A (Continued)

ACCOUNT Electricity Expense   ACCOUNT NO. 533

DATE	ITEM	POST. REF.	DEBIT	CREDIT	BALANCE DEBIT	BALANCE CREDIT

ACCOUNT Charitable Contributions Expense   ACCOUNT NO. 534

DATE	ITEM	POST. REF.	DEBIT	CREDIT	BALANCE DEBIT	BALANCE CREDIT

ACCOUNT Gas and Oil Expense   ACCOUNT NO. 538

DATE	ITEM	POST. REF.	DEBIT	CREDIT	BALANCE DEBIT	BALANCE CREDIT

ACCOUNT Miscellaneous Expense   ACCOUNT NO. 549

DATE	ITEM	POST. REF.	DEBIT	CREDIT	BALANCE DEBIT	BALANCE CREDIT

Problem 4-9A (Concluded)

4.

_____

_____

_____

ACCOUNT	ACCT. NO.	DEBIT BALANCE	CREDIT BALANCE

Problem 4-10A
2. (For 1. & 3., see page WP-69)

GENERAL JOURNAL   PAGE   1

	DATE		DESCRIPTION	POST. REF.	DEBIT	CREDIT	
1							1
2							2
3							3
4							4
5							5
6							6
7							7
8							8
9							9
10							10
11							11
12							12
13							13
14							14
15							15
16							16
17							17
18							18
19							19
20							20
21							21
22							22
23							23
24							24
25							25
26							26
27							27
28							28
29							29
30							30
31							31
32							32
33							33
34							34
35							35
36							36

Problem 4-10A (Continued)

GENERAL JOURNAL

	DATE	DESCRIPTION	POST. REF.	DEBIT	CREDIT	
1						1
2						2
3						3
4						4
5						5
6						6
7						7
8						8
9						9
10						10
11						11
12						12
13						13
14						14
15						15
16						16
17						17
18						18
19						19
20						20
21						21
22						22
23						23
24						24
25						25
26						26
27						27
28						28
29						29
30						30
31						31
32						32
33						33
34						34
35						35
36						36

Problem 4-10A (Continued)

GENERAL JOURNAL

	DATE		DESCRIPTION	POST. REF.	DEBIT	CREDIT	
1							1
2							2
3							3
4							4
5							5
6							6
7							7
8							8
9							9
10							10
11							11
12							12
13							13
14							14
15							15
16							16
17							17
18							18
19							19
20							20
21							21
22							22
23							23
24							24
25							25
26							26
27							27
28							28
29							29
30							30
31							31
32							32
33							33
34							34
35							35
36							36

Problem 4-10A (Continued)

1. & 3.

GENERAL LEDGER

ACCOUNT Cash   ACCOUNT NO. 101

DATE	ITEM	POST. REF.	DEBIT	CREDIT	BALANCE	
					DEBIT	CREDIT

ACCOUNT Office Supplies   ACCOUNT NO. 142

DATE	ITEM	POST. REF.	DEBIT	CREDIT	BALANCE	
					DEBIT	CREDIT

Problem 4-10A (Continued)

ACCOUNT Office Equipment   ACCOUNT NO. 181

DATE	ITEM	POST. REF.	DEBIT	CREDIT	BALANCE DEBIT	BALANCE CREDIT

ACCOUNT Accounts Payable   ACCOUNT NO. 202

DATE	ITEM	POST. REF.	DEBIT	CREDIT	BALANCE DEBIT	BALANCE CREDIT

ACCOUNT Annette Creighton, Capital   ACCOUNT NO. 311

DATE	ITEM	POST. REF.	DEBIT	CREDIT	BALANCE DEBIT	BALANCE CREDIT

ACCOUNT Annette Creighton, Drawing   ACCOUNT NO. 312

DATE	ITEM	POST. REF.	DEBIT	CREDIT	BALANCE DEBIT	BALANCE CREDIT

Problem 4-10A (Continued)

ACCOUNT Consulting Fees   ACCOUNT NO. 401

DATE	ITEM	POST. REF.	DEBIT	CREDIT	BALANCE DEBIT	BALANCE CREDIT

ACCOUNT Wages Expense   ACCOUNT NO. 511

DATE	ITEM	POST. REF.	DEBIT	CREDIT	BALANCE DEBIT	BALANCE CREDIT

ACCOUNT Advertising Expense   ACCOUNT NO. 512

DATE	ITEM	POST. REF.	DEBIT	CREDIT	BALANCE DEBIT	BALANCE CREDIT

ACCOUNT Rent Expense   ACCOUNT NO. 521

DATE	ITEM	POST. REF.	DEBIT	CREDIT	BALANCE DEBIT	BALANCE CREDIT

Problem 4-10A (Continued)

ACCOUNT Telephone Expense   ACCOUNT NO. 525

DATE	ITEM	POST. REF.	DEBIT	CREDIT	BALANCE DEBIT	BALANCE CREDIT

ACCOUNT Transportation Expense   ACCOUNT NO. 526

DATE	ITEM	POST. REF.	DEBIT	CREDIT	BALANCE DEBIT	BALANCE CREDIT

ACCOUNT Utilities Expense   ACCOUNT NO. 533

DATE	ITEM	POST. REF.	DEBIT	CREDIT	BALANCE DEBIT	BALANCE CREDIT

ACCOUNT Miscellaneous Expense   ACCOUNT NO. 549

DATE	ITEM	POST. REF.	DEBIT	CREDIT	BALANCE DEBIT	BALANCE CREDIT

Problem 4-10A (Continued)

4.

ACCOUNT	ACCT. NO.	DEBIT BALANCE	CREDIT BALANCE

Problem 4-10A (Continued)

5.

Exercise 4-5B (Continued)

ACCOUNT _____   ACCOUNT NO. _____

DATE		ITEM	POST. REF.	DEBIT	CREDIT	BALANCE	
						DEBIT	CREDIT

ACCOUNT _____   ACCOUNT NO. _____

DATE		ITEM	POST. REF.	DEBIT	CREDIT	BALANCE	
						DEBIT	CREDIT

ACCOUNT _____   ACCOUNT NO. _____

DATE		ITEM	POST. REF.	DEBIT	CREDIT	BALANCE	
						DEBIT	CREDIT

ACCOUNT _____   ACCOUNT NO. _____

DATE		ITEM	POST. REF.	DEBIT	CREDIT	BALANCE	
						DEBIT	CREDIT

Exercise 4-5B (Continued)

ACCOUNT _____ ACCOUNT NO. _____

DATE	ITEM	POST. REF.	DEBIT	CREDIT	BALANCE	
					DEBIT	CREDIT

ACCOUNT _____ ACCOUNT NO. _____

DATE	ITEM	POST. REF.	DEBIT	CREDIT	BALANCE	
					DEBIT	CREDIT

ACCOUNT _____ ACCOUNT NO. _____

DATE	ITEM	POST. REF.	DEBIT	CREDIT	BALANCE	
					DEBIT	CREDIT

ACCOUNT _____ ACCOUNT NO. _____

DATE	ITEM	POST. REF.	DEBIT	CREDIT	BALANCE	
					DEBIT	CREDIT

ACCOUNT _____ ACCOUNT NO. _____

DATE	ITEM	POST. REF.	DEBIT	CREDIT	BALANCE	
					DEBIT	CREDIT

Exercise 4-5B (Concluded)

ACCOUNT	ACCT. NO.	DEBIT BALANCE	CREDIT BALANCE

Exercise 4-6B

Exercise 4-6B (Concluded)

Name _____

Exercise 4-7B

Exercise 4-7B (Concluded)

Exercise 4-8B

GENERAL JOURNAL

PAGE

	DATE		DESCRIPTION	POST. REF.	DEBIT	CREDIT	
15	Apr.	6	Office Supplies		5 3 0 00		15
16			Cash			5 3 0 00	16
17			Purchased office equipment				17
18							18
23		21	Cash	101	3 0 0 00		23
24			Service Fees	401		3 0 0 00	24
25			Revenue earned from services.				25
26							26
27							27
28							28
29							29
30							30
31							31
32							32
33							33

Problem 4-9B

2. (For 1. & 3., see page WP-90)

GENERAL JOURNAL   PAGE 7

	DATE		DESCRIPTION	POST. REF.	DEBIT	CREDIT	
1							1
2							2
3							3
4							4
5							5
6							6
7							7
8							8
9							9
10							10
11							11
12							12
13							13
14							14
15							15
16							16
17							17
18							18
19							19
20							20
21							21
22							22
23							23
24							24
25							25
26							26
27							27
28							28
29							29
30							30
31							31
32							32
33							33
34							34

Problem 4-9B (Continued)

GENERAL JOURNAL

	DATE		DESCRIPTION	POST. REF.	DEBIT	CREDIT	
1							1
2							2
3							3
4							4
5							5
6							6
7							7
8							8
9							9
10							10
11							11
12							12
13							13
14							14
15							15
16							16
17							17
18							18
19							19
20							20
21							21
22							22
23							23
24							24
25							25
26							26
27							27
28							28
29							29
30							30
31							31
32							32
33							33
34							34
35							35
36							36

Problem 4-9B (Continued)

GENERAL JOURNAL   PAGE 9

	DATE		DESCRIPTION	POST. REF.	DEBIT	CREDIT	
1							1
2							2
3							3
4							4
5							5
6							6
7							7
8							8
9							9
10							10
11							11
12							12
13							13
14							14
15							15
16							16
17							17
18							0
19							19
20							20
21							21
22							22
23							23
24							24
25							25
26							26
27							27
28							28
29							29
30							30
31							31
32							32
33							33
34							34
35							35
36							36

Problem 4-9B (Continued)

1. & 3.

GENERAL LEDGER

ACCOUNT Cash   ACCOUNT NO. 101

DATE	ITEM	POST. REF.	DEBIT	CREDIT	BALANCE DEBIT	BALANCE CREDIT

ACCOUNT Accounts Receivable   ACCOUNT NO. 122

DATE	ITEM	POST. REF.	DEBIT	CREDIT	BALANCE DEBIT	BALANCE CREDIT

Problem 4-9B (Continued)

ACCOUNT Tailoring Supplies   ACCOUNT NO. 141

DATE	ITEM	POST. REF.	DEBIT	CREDIT	BALANCE DEBIT	BALANCE CREDIT

ACCOUNT Tailoring Equipment   ACCOUNT NO. 183

DATE	ITEM	POST. REF.	DEBIT	CREDIT	BALANCE DEBIT	BALANCE CREDIT

ACCOUNT Accounts Payable   ACCOUNT NO. 202

DATE	ITEM	POST. REF.	DEBIT	CREDIT	BALANCE DEBIT	BALANCE CREDIT

ACCOUNT Ann Tailor , Capital   ACCOUNT NO. 311

DATE	ITEM	POST. REF.	DEBIT	CREDIT	BALANCE DEBIT	BALANCE CREDIT

Problem 4-9B (Continued)

ACCOUNT Ann Tailor, Drawing   ACCOUNT NO. 312

DATE	ITEM	POST. REF.	DEBIT	CREDIT	BALANCE	
					DEBIT	CREDIT

ACCOUNT Tailoring Fees   ACCOUNT NO. 401

DATE	ITEM	POST. REF.	DEBIT	CREDIT	BALANCE	
					DEBIT	CREDIT

ACCOUNT Wages Expense   ACCOUNT NO. 511

DATE	ITEM	POST. REF.	DEBIT	CREDIT	BALANCE	
					DEBIT	CREDIT

ACCOUNT Advertising Expense   ACCOUNT NO. 512

DATE	ITEM	POST. REF.	DEBIT	CREDIT	BALANCE	
					DEBIT	CREDIT

Problem 4-9B (Continued)

ACCOUNT Rent Expense   ACCOUNT NO. 521

DATE	ITEM	POST. REF.	DEBIT	CREDIT	BALANCE DEBIT	BALANCE CREDIT

ACCOUNT Telephone Expense   ACCOUNT NO. 525

DATE	ITEM	POST. REF.	DEBIT	CREDIT	BALANCE DEBIT	BALANCE CREDIT

ACCOUNT Electricity Expense   ACCOUNT NO. 533

DATE	ITEM	POST. REF.	DEBIT	CREDIT	BALANCE DEBIT	BALANCE CREDIT

ACCOUNT Miscellaneous Expense   ACCOUNT NO. 549

DATE	ITEM	POST. REF.	DEBIT	CREDIT	BALANCE DEBIT	BALANCE CREDIT

Problem 4-9B (Concluded)

4.

ACCOUNT	ACCT. NO.	DEBIT BALANCE	CREDIT BALANCE

Mastery Problem

1.

GENERAL JOURNAL

	DATE	DESCRIPTION	POST. REF.	DEBIT	CREDIT	
1						1
2						2
3						3
4						4
5						5
6						6
7						7
8						8
9						9
10						10
11						11
12						12
13						13
14						14
15						15
16						16
17						17
18						18
19						19
20						20
21						21
22						22
23						23
24						24
25						25
26						26
27						27
28						28
29						29
30						30
31						31
32						32
33						33
34						34
35						35

Mastery Problem (Continued)

GENERAL JOURNAL

PAGE 2

	DATE		DESCRIPTION	POST. REF.	DEBIT	CREDIT	
1							1
2							2
3							3
4							4
5							5
6							6
7							7
8							8
9							9
10							10
11							11
12							12
13							13
14							14
15							15
16							16
17							17
18							18
19							19
20							20
21							21
22							22
23							23
24							24
25							25
26							26
27							27
28							28
29							29
30							30
31							31
32							32
33							33
34							34
35							35

Mastery Problem (Continued)

GENERAL JOURNAL

	DATE		DESCRIPTION	POST. REF.	DEBIT	CREDIT	
1							1
2							2
3							3
4							4
5							5
6							6
7							7
8							8
9							9
10							10
11							11
12							12
13							13
14							14
15							15
16							16
17							17
18							18
19							19
20							20
21							21
22							22
23							23
24							24
25							25
26							26
27							27
28							28
29							29
30							30
31							31
32							32
33							33
34							34
35							35

Mastery Problem (Continued)

2.

ACCOUNT   Cash   ACCOUNT NO.   101

DATE	ITEM	POST. REF.	DEBIT	CREDIT	BALANCE	
					DEBIT	CREDIT

ACCOUNT Office Supplies   ACCOUNT NO. 142

DATE	ITEM	POST. REF.	DEBIT	CREDIT	BALANCE	
					DEBIT	CREDIT

ACCOUNT   Athletic Equipment   ACCOUNT NO.   183

DATE	ITEM	POST. REF.	DEBIT	CREDIT	BALANCE	
					DEBIT	CREDIT

Mastery Problem (Continued)

ACCOUNT Basketball Facilities   ACCOUNT NO. 184

DATE	ITEM	POST. REF.	DEBIT	CREDIT	BALANCE	
					DEBIT	CREDIT

ACCOUNT Accounts Payable   ACCOUNT NO. 202

DATE	ITEM	POST. REF.	DEBIT	CREDIT	BALANCE	
					DEBIT	CREDIT

ACCOUNT Barry Bird, Capital   ACCOUNT NO. 311

DATE	ITEM	POST. REF.	DEBIT	CREDIT	BALANCE	
					DEBIT	CREDIT

ACCOUNT Barry Bird, Drawing   ACCOUNT NO. 312

DATE	ITEM	POST. REF.	DEBIT	CREDIT	BALANCE	
					DEBIT	CREDIT

Mastery Problem (Continued)

ACCOUNT Registration Fees   ACCOUNT NO. 401

DATE	ITEM	POST. REF.	DEBIT	CREDIT	BALANCE	
					DEBIT	CREDIT

ACCOUNT Wages Expense   ACCOUNT NO. 511

DATE	ITEM	POST. REF.	DEBIT	CREDIT	BALANCE	
					DEBIT	CREDIT

ACCOUNT Advertising Expense   ACCOUNT NO. 512

DATE	ITEM	POST. REF.	DEBIT	CREDIT	BALANCE	
					DEBIT	CREDIT

Mastery Problem (Continued)

ACCOUNT Food Expense   ACCOUNT NO. 524

DATE		ITEM	POST. REF.	DEBIT	CREDIT	BALANCE	
						DEBIT	CREDIT

ACCOUNT Telephone Expense   ACCOUNT NO. 525

DATE		ITEM	POST. REF.	DEBIT	CREDIT	BALANCE	
						DEBIT	CREDIT

ACCOUNT Utilities Expense   ACCOUNT NO. 533

DATE		ITEM	POST. REF.	DEBIT	CREDIT	BALANCE	
						DEBIT	CREDIT

ACCOUNT Postage Expense   ACCOUNT NO. 536

DATE		ITEM	POST. REF.	DEBIT	CREDIT	BALANCE	
						DEBIT	CREDIT

Mastery Problem (Concluded)

ACCOUNT	ACCT. NO.	DEBIT BALANCE	CREDIT BALANCE

Challenge Problem

Fred Phaler Consulting

Trial Balance

June 30, 20--

ACCOUNT	ACCT. NO.	DEBIT BALANCE	CREDIT BALANCE
Cash	101		
Accounts Receivable	122		
Office Supplies	142		
Accounts Payable	202		
Fred Phaler, Capital	311		
Fred Phaler, Drawing	312		
Professional Fees	401		
Wages Expense	511		
Rent Expense	521		
Telephone Expense	525		
Automobile Expense	526		
Utilities Expense	533		

Exercise 5-1A

(Balance Sheet) Supplies	(Income Statement) Supplies Expense

GENERAL JOURNAL PAGE ____

	DATE	DESCRIPTION	POST. REF.	DEBIT	CREDIT	
1						1
2						2
3						3
4						4
5						5
6						6

Exercise 5-2A

(Balance Sheet) Prepaid Insurance	(Income Statement) Insurance Expense
900 150	150

$$\frac{900}{6} = 150$$

6 mos

GENERAL JOURNAL PAGE ____

	DATE	DESCRIPTION	POST. REF.	DEBIT	CREDIT	
1	2007 Dec 1	Ins Exp		15000		1
2		Prepaid Ins			15000	2
3						3
4						4
5						5
6						6

Exercise 5-3A

(Income Statement) Wages Expense	(Balance Sheet) Wages Payable
600 200 ——— 800	200

GENERAL JOURNAL   PAGE

	DATE	DESCRIPTION	POST. REF.	DEBIT	CREDIT	
1	2007 Dec 31	Wages Exp		200 00		1
2		Wages Pay			200 00	2
3						3
4						4

Exercise 5-4A

Original cost _____ × Salvage Value = 7200

(Income Statement) Depr. Expense—Delivery Equip.	(Balance Sheet) Accum. Depr.—Delivery Equip.
150 7200 48 = 150	150

GENERAL JOURNAL   PAGE

	DATE	DESCRIPTION	POST. REF.	DEBIT	CREDIT	
1	2007 Dec 31	Depreciating Expense		150 00		1
2		Acc Dep - Del Eq.			150 00	2
3						3
4						4

Exercise 5-5A

_____

_____

_____

Exercise 5-6A

1.

| (Balance Sheet) Supplies | (Income Statement) Supplies Expense |

2.

| (Balance Sheet) Supplies | (Income Statement) Supplies Expense |

Exercise 5-7A

1.

| (Balance Sheet) Prepaid Insurance | (Income Statement) Insurance Expense |

2.

| (Balance Sheet) Prepaid Insurance | (Income Statement) Insurance Expense |

Exercise 5-8A

Jim Jacob's Furniture Repair

Work Sheet (Partial)

For Year Ended December 31, 20--

	DESCRIPTION	TRIAL BALANCE DEBIT	TRIAL BALANCE CREDIT	ADJUSTMENTS DEBIT	ADJUSTMENTS CREDIT	ADJUSTED TRIAL BALANCE DEBIT	ADJUSTED TRIAL BALANCE CREDIT	
1	Cash	1 0 0 00				1 0 0 00		1
2	Supplies	8 5 0 00				2 0 0 00		2
3	Prepaid Insurance	9 0 0 00				3 0 0 00		3
4	Delivery Equipment	3 6 0 0 00				3 6 0 0 00		4
5	Accum. Depr.—Delivery Equip.		6 0 0 00				8 0 0 00	5
6	Wages Payable						1 0 0 00	6
7	Jim Jacob, Capital		4 0 0 0 00				4 0 0 0 00	7
8	Repair Fees		1 6 5 0 00				1 6 5 0 00	8
9	Wages Expense	6 0 0 00				7 0 0 00		9
10	Advertising Expense	2 0 0 00				2 0 0 00		10
11	Supplies Expense					6 5 0 00		11
12	Insurance Expense					6 0 0 00		12
13	Depr. Exp.—Delivery Equip.					2 0 0 00		13
14		6 2 5 0 00	6 2 5 0 00			6 5 5 0 00	6 5 5 0 00	14
15								15
16								16
17								17
18								18
19								19
20								20
21								21
22								22
23								23
24								24
25								25

Exercise 5-9A

GENERAL JOURNAL PAGE _____

DATE		DESCRIPTION	POST. REF.	DEBIT	CREDIT	
1						1
2						2
3						3
4						4
5						5
6						6
7						7
8						8
9						9
10						10
11						11
12						12
13						13
14						14
15						15

Exercise 5-10A

	Income Statement		Balance Sheet	
	Debit	**Credit**	**Debit**	**Credit**
Cash				
Accounts Receivable				
Supplies				
Prepaid Insurance				
Delivery Equipment				
Accum. Depr.—Del. Equip.				
Accounts Payable				
Wages Payable				
Owner, Capital				
Owner, Drawing				
Delivery Fees				
Wages Expense				
Rent Expense				

Exercise 5-10A (Continued)

| | Income Statement | | Balance Sheet | |
	Debit	Credit	Debit	Credit
Supplies Expense				
Insurance Expense				
Depr. Exp.—Del. Equip.				

Exercise 5-11A

| | Income Statement | | Balance Sheet | |
	Debit	Credit	Debit	Credit
Net Income				
Net Loss				

Exercise 5-12A

GENERAL JOURNAL

PAGE 9

	DATE		DESCRIPTION	POST. REF.	DEBIT	CREDIT	
1	20-- Dec.		Adjusting Entries				1
2		31	Supplies Expense		8 5 00		2
3			Supplies			8 5 00	3
4							4
5		31	Wages Expense		2 2 0 00		5
6			Wages Payable			2 2 0 00	6
7							7
8							8
9							9
10							10
11							11
12							12
13							13
14							14
15							15
16							16
17							17
18							18

Exercise 5-12A (Concluded)

GENERAL LEDGER

ACCOUNT Supplies   ACCOUNT NO. 141

DATE		ITEM	POST. REF.	DEBIT	CREDIT	BALANCE	
						DEBIT	CREDIT
20-- Dec.	1	Balance	✓			1 5 0 00	
	15		J8	5 0 00		2 0 0 00	

ACCOUNT Wages Payable   ACCOUNT NO. 219

DATE	ITEM	POST. REF.	DEBIT	CREDIT	BALANCE	
					DEBIT	CREDIT

ACCOUNT Wages Expense   ACCOUNT NO. 511

DATE		ITEM	POST. REF.	DEBIT	CREDIT	BALANCE	
						DEBIT	CREDIT
20-- Dec.	1	Balance	✓			9 0 0 00	
	15		J8	3 0 0 00		1 2 0 0 00	

ACCOUNT Supplies Expense   ACCOUNT NO. 523

DATE	ITEM	POST. REF.	DEBIT	CREDIT	BALANCE	
					DEBIT	CREDIT

Problem 5-13A

Mason's Delivery

Work

For Month Ended

	ACCOUNT TITLE	TRIAL BALANCE			ADJUSTMENTS		
		DEBIT	CREDIT		DEBIT	CREDIT	
1	Cash	1 6 0 0 00					
2	Accounts Receivable	9 4 0 00					
3	Supplies	6 3 5 00					
4	Prepaid Insurance	1 2 0 0 00					
5	Delivery Equipment	6 4 0 0 00					
6	Accum. Depr.—Delivery Equip.						
7	Accounts Payable		1 2 2 0 00				
8	Wages Payable						
9	Jill Mason, Capital		8 0 0 0 00				
10	Jill Mason, Drawing	1 4 0 0 00					
11	Delivery Fees		6 2 0 0 00				
12	Wages Expense	1 5 0 0 00					
13	Advertising Expense	4 6 0 00					
14	Rent Expense	8 0 0 00					
15	Supplies Expense						
16	Telephone Expense	1 6 5 00					
17	Insurance Expense						
18	Repair Expense	2 3 0 00					
19	Oil & Gas Expense	9 0 00					
20	Depr. Exp.—Delivery Equip.						
21		15 4 2 0 00	15 4 2 0 00				
22							
23							
24							
25							
26							
27							
28							
29							
30							
31							
32							
33							

Problem 5-13A (Concluded)

Service

Sheet

September 30, 20--

ADJUSTED TRIAL BALANCE		INCOME STATEMENT		BALANCE SHEET		
DEBIT	CREDIT	DEBIT	CREDIT	DEBIT	CREDIT	
						1
						2
						3
						4
						5
						6
						7
						8
						9
						10
						11
						12
						13
						14
						15
						16
						17
						18
						19
						20
						21
						22
						23
						24
						25
						26
						27
						28
						29
						30
						31
						32
						33

Problem 5-14A

Campus Escort

Work

For Month Ended

	ACCOUNT TITLE	TRIAL BALANCE			ADJUSTMENTS		
		DEBIT		CREDIT		DEBIT	CREDIT
1	Cash	9 8 0 00					
2	Accounts Receivable	5 9 0 00					
3	Supplies	5 7 5 00					(a) 3 9 0 00
4	Prepaid Insurance	1 3 0 0 00					(b) 5 0 0 00
5	Van	5 8 0 0 00					
6	Accumulated Depreciation—Van						(c) 3 0 0 00
7	Accounts Payable			9 6 0 00			
8	Wages Payable						(d) 1 9 0 00
9	Jason Armstrong, Capital			10 0 0 0 00			
10	Jason Armstrong, Drawing	6 0 0 00					
11	Escort Fees			2 6 0 0 00			
12	Wages Expense	1 8 0 0 00				(d) 1 9 0 00	
13	Advertising Expense	3 8 0 00					
14	Rent Expense	9 0 0 00					
15	Supplies Expense					(a) 3 9 0 00	
16	Telephone Expense	2 2 0 00					
17	Insurance Expense				(b) 5 0 0 00		
18	Repair Expense	3 1 5 00					
19	Oil and Gas Expense	1 0 0 00					
20	Depreciation Expense—Van				(c) 3 0 0 00		
21		13 5 6 0 00		13 5 6 0 00			
22							
23							
24							
25							
26							
27							
28							
29							
30							
31							
32							
33							

Name _____

Problem 5-14A (Concluded)

Service _____

Sheet _____

November 30, 20-- _____

ADJUSTED TRIAL BALANCE		INCOME STATEMENT		BALANCE SHEET		
DEBIT	CREDIT	DEBIT	CREDIT	DEBIT	CREDIT	
						1
						2
						3
						4
						5
						6
						7
						8
						9
						10
						11
						12
						13
						14
						15
						16
						17
						18
						19
						20
						21
						22
						23
						24
						25
						26
						27
						28
						29
						30
						31
						32
						33

Problem 5-15A

GENERAL JOURNAL PAGE 5

	DATE		DESCRIPTION	POST. REF.	DEBIT	CREDIT	
1							1
2							2
3							3
4							4
5							5
6							6
7							7
8							8
9							9
10							10
11							11
12							12
13							13
14							14
15							15
16							16
17							17
18							18
19							19
20							20
21							21
22							22
23							23
24							24
25							25
26							26
27							27
28							28
29							29
30							30
31							31
32							32
33							33
34							34
35							35
36							36

Problem 5-15A (Continued)

GENERAL LEDGER

ACCOUNT Supplies   ACCOUNT NO. 141

DATE		ITEM	POST. REF.	DEBIT	CREDIT	BALANCE	
						DEBIT	CREDIT
20-- Nov.	1		J1	4 7 5 00		4 7 5 00	
	15		J4	1 0 0 00		5 7 5 00	

ACCOUNT Prepaid Insurance   ACCOUNT NO. 145

DATE		ITEM	POST. REF.	DEBIT	CREDIT	BALANCE	
						DEBIT	CREDIT
20-- Nov.	1		J1	1 3 0 0 00		1 3 0 0 00	

ACCOUNT Accumulated Depreciation—Van   ACCOUNT NO. 185.1

DATE	ITEM	POST. REF.	DEBIT	CREDIT	BALANCE	
					DEBIT	CREDIT

ACCOUNT Wages Payable   ACCOUNT NO. 219

DATE	ITEM	POST. REF.	DEBIT	CREDIT	BALANCE	
					DEBIT	CREDIT

Problem 5-15A (Concluded)

GENERAL LEDGER

ACCOUNT Wages Expense   ACCOUNT NO. 511

DATE		ITEM	POST. REF.	DEBIT	CREDIT	BALANCE	
						DEBIT	CREDIT
20-- Nov.	15		J3	9 0 0 00		9 0 0 00	
	26		J4	9 0 0 00		1 8 0 0 00	

ACCOUNT Supplies Expense   ACCOUNT NO. 523

DATE	ITEM	POST. REF.	DEBIT	CREDIT	BALANCE	
					DEBIT	CREDIT

ACCOUNT Insurance Expense   ACCOUNT NO. 535

DATE	ITEM	POST. REF.	DEBIT	CREDIT	BALANCE	
					DEBIT	CREDIT

ACCOUNT Depreciation Expense—Van   ACCOUNT NO. 541

DATE	ITEM	POST. REF.	DEBIT	CREDIT	BALANCE	
					DEBIT	CREDIT

Problem 5-16A: See pages 130 and 131

Exercise 5-1B

(Balance Sheet)
Supplies

(Income Statement)
Supplies Expense

GENERAL JOURNAL   PAGE

	DATE	DESCRIPTION	POST. REF.	DEBIT	CREDIT	
1						1
2						2
3						3
4						4
5						5
6						6

Exercise 5-2B

(Balance Sheet)
Prepaid Insurance

(Income Statement)
Insurance Expense

GENERAL JOURNAL   PAGE

	DATE	DESCRIPTION	POST. REF.	DEBIT	CREDIT	
1						1
2						2
3						3
4						4
5						5
6						6

Problem 5-16A

Joyce Lee's

Work

For Month Ended

	ACCOUNT TITLE	TRIAL BALANCE										ADJUSTMENTS							
		DEBIT					CREDIT					DEBIT				CREDIT			
1	Cash	1	7	2	5	00													
2	Accounts Receivable		9	6	0	00													
3	Supplies		5	2	5	00													
4	Prepaid Insurance		9	3	0	00													
5	Office Equipment	5	4	5	0	00													
6	Accum. Depr.—Office Equipment																		
7	Accounts Payable							4	8	0	00								
8	Wages Payable																		
9	Joyce Lee, Capital						7	5	0	0	00								
10	Joyce Lee, Drawing	1	1	2	5	00													
11	Professional Fees						5	7	0	0	00								
12	Wages Expense	1	4	2	0	00													
13	Advertising Expense		3	5	0	00													
14	Rent Expense		7	0	0	00													
15	Supplies Expense																		
16	Telephone Expense		1	3	0	00													
17	Utilities Expense		1	9	0	00													
18	Insurance Expense																		
19	Depr. Expense—Office Equipment																		
20	Miscellaneous Expense		1	7	5	00													
21		13	6	8	0	00	13	6	8	0	00								
22																			
23																			
24																			
25																			
26																			
27																			
28																			
29																			
30																			
31																			
32																			
33																			

Exercise 5-6B

1.

| (Balance Sheet) | (Income Statement) |
| Supplies | Supplies Expense |

2.

| (Balance Sheet) | (Income Statement) |
| Supplies | Supplies Expense |

Exercise 5-7B

1.

| (Balance Sheet) | (Income Statement) |
| Prepaid Insurance | Insurance Expense |

2.

| (Balance Sheet) | (Income Statement) |
| Prepaid Insurance | Insurance Expense |

Exercise 5-8B

Jasmine Kah's Auto Detailing
Work Sheet (Partial)
For Month Ended June 30, 20--

#	DESCRIPTION	TRIAL BALANCE DEBIT	TRIAL BALANCE CREDIT	ADJUSTMENTS DEBIT	ADJUSTMENTS CREDIT	ADJUSTED TRIAL BALANCE DEBIT	ADJUSTED TRIAL BALANCE CREDIT
1	Cash	1 5 0 00				1 5 0 00	
2	Supplies	5 2 0 00				9 0 00	
3	Prepaid Insurance	7 5 0 00				2 0 0 00	
4	Cleaning Equipment	5 4 0 0 00				5 4 0 0 00	
5	Accum. Depr.—Cleaning Equip.		8 5 0 00				1 1 5 0 00
6	Wages Payable						2 5 0 00
7	Jasmine Kah, Capital		4 6 0 0 00				4 6 0 0 00
8	Detailing Fees		2 2 2 0 00				2 2 2 0 00
9	Wages Expense	7 0 0 00				9 5 0 00	
10	Advertising Expense	1 5 0 00				1 5 0 00	
11	Supplies Expense					4 3 0 00	
12	Insurance Expense					5 5 0 00	
13	Depr. Exp.—Cleaning Equip.					3 0 0 00	
14		7 6 7 0 00	7 6 7 0 00			8 2 2 0 00	8 2 2 0 00
15							
16							
17							
18							
19							
20							
21							
22							
23							
24							
25							

Exercise 5-9B

GENERAL JOURNAL

PAGE ____

	DATE		DESCRIPTION	POST. REF.	DEBIT	CREDIT	
1							1
2							2
3							3
4							4
5							5
6							6
7							7
8							8
9							9
10							10
11							11
12							12
13							13
14							14
15							15

Exercise 5-10B

	Income Statement		Balance Sheet	
	Debit	**Credit**	**Debit**	**Credit**
Cash				
Accounts Receivable				
Supplies				
Prepaid Insurance				
Automobile				
Accum. Depr.—Automobile				
Accounts Payable				
Wages Payable				
Owner, Capital				
Owner, Drawing				
Service Fees				
Wages Expense				
Supplies Expense				

Exercise 5-10B (Concluded)

	Income Statement		Balance Sheet	
	Debit	**Credit**	**Debit**	**Credit**
Utilities Expense	_____	_____	_____	_____
Insurance Expense	_____	_____	_____	_____
Depr. Exp.—Automobile	_____	_____	_____	_____

Exercise 5-11B

	Income Statement		Balance Sheet	
	Debit	**Credit**	**Debit**	**Credit**
Net Income	_____	_____	_____	_____
Net Loss	_____	_____	_____	_____

Exercise 5-12B

GENERAL JOURNAL

PAGE 7

	DATE		DESCRIPTION	POST. REF.	DEBIT	CREDIT	
1			Adjusting Entries				1
2	20-- July	31	Insurance Expense		3 2 0 00		2
3			Prepaid Insurance			3 2 0 00	3
4							4
5		31	Depreciation Expense—Cleaning Equipment		1 4 5 00		5
6			Accumulated Depreciation—Cleaning Equipment			1 4 5 00	6
7							7
8							8
9							9
10							10
11							11
12							12
13							13
14							14
15							15
16							16

Exercise 5-12B (Concluded)

GENERAL LEDGER

ACCOUNT Prepaid Insurance   ACCOUNT NO. 145

DATE		ITEM	POST. REF.	DEBIT	CREDIT	BALANCE DEBIT	BALANCE CREDIT
20-- July	1	Balance	✓			3 2 0 00	
	15		J6	6 4 0 00		9 6 0 00	

ACCOUNT Accumulated Depreciation—Cleaning Equip.   ACCOUNT NO. 183.1

DATE		ITEM	POST. REF.	DEBIT	CREDIT	BALANCE DEBIT	BALANCE CREDIT
20-- July	1	Balance	✓				8 7 0 00

ACCOUNT Insurance Expense   ACCOUNT NO. 535

DATE		ITEM	POST. REF.	DEBIT	CREDIT	BALANCE DEBIT	BALANCE CREDIT

ACCOUNT Depreciation Expense—Cleaning Equip.   ACCOUNT NO. 541

DATE		ITEM	POST. REF.	DEBIT	CREDIT	BALANCE DEBIT	BALANCE CREDIT

Problem 5-13B

Louie's Lawn

Work

For Month Ended

	ACCOUNT TITLE	TRIAL BALANCE										ADJUSTMENTS										
		DEBIT					CREDIT					DEBIT					CREDIT					
1	Cash	1	3	7	5	00																
2	Accounts Receivable		8	8	0	00																
3	Supplies		4	9	0	00																
4	Prepaid Insurance		8	0	0	00																
5	Lawn Equipment	5	7	0	0	00																
6	Accum. Depr.—Lawn Equipment																					
7	Accounts Payable							7	8	0	00											
8	Wages Payable																					
9	Louie Long, Capital						6	5	0	0	00											
10	Louie Long, Drawing	1	2	5	0	00																
11	Lawn Service Fees						6	1	0	0	00											
12	Wages Expense	1	1	4	5	00																
13	Advertising Expense		5	4	0	00																
14	Rent Expense		7	2	5	00																
15	Supplies Expense																					
16	Telephone Expense		1	6	0	00																
17	Insurance Expense																					
18	Repair Expense		2	5	0	00																
19	Depr. Expense—Lawn Equipment																					
20	Miscellaneous Expense			6	5	00																
21		13	3	8	0	00	13	3	8	0	00											
22																						
23																						
24																						
25																						
26																						
27																						
28																						
29																						
30																						
31																						
32																						
33																						

Mastery Problem (Continued)

Counseling Services

Sheet

December 31, 20--

ADJUSTED TRIAL BALANCE		INCOME STATEMENT		BALANCE SHEET		
DEBIT	CREDIT	DEBIT	CREDIT	DEBIT	CREDIT	
						1
						2
						3
						4
						5
						6
						7
						8
						9
						10
						11
						12
						13
						14
						15
						16
						17
						18
						19
						20
						21
						22
						23
						24
						25
						26
						27
						28
						29
						30
						31
						32

Mastery Problem (Concluded)

2.

GENERAL JOURNAL

	DATE		DESCRIPTION	POST. REF.	DEBIT	CREDIT	
1							1
2							2
3							3
4							4
5							5
6							6
7							7
8							8
9							9
10							10
11							11
12							12
13							13
14							14
15							15
16							16
17							17
18							18
19							19
20							20
21							21
22							22
23							23
24							24
25							25
26							26
27							27
28							28
29							29
30							30
31							31
32							32
33							33
34							34
35							35

Challenge Problem

See pages 152-153 for work sheet for Challenge Problem.

Challenge Problem

1.

Diane Kiefner's Wilderness

Work

For Summer

	ACCOUNT TITLE	TRIAL BALANCE												ADJUSTMENTS										
		DEBIT					CREDIT						DEBIT					CREDIT						
1	Cash	11	5	0	0	00																		
2																								
3																								
4																								
5	Diane Kiefner, Capital						15	0	0	0	00													
6	Tour Revenue						10	0	0	0	00													
7	Advertising Supplies Expense	1	0	0	0	00																		
8	Food Expense	2	0	0	0	00																		
9	Equipment Rental Expense	3	0	0	0	00																		
10	Travel Expense	4	0	0	0	00																		
11	Kayak Expense	3	5	0	0	00																		
12																								
13		25	0	0	0	00	25	0	0	0	00													
14																								
15																								
16																								
17																								
18																								
19																								

Challenge Problem (Concluded)

Kayaking Tours _____

Sheet _____

Ended 20-- _____

	ADJUSTED TRIAL BALANCE		INCOME STATEMENT		BALANCE SHEET		
	DEBIT	CREDIT	DEBIT	CREDIT	DEBIT	CREDIT	
							1
							2
							3
							4
							5
							6
							7
							8
							9
							10
							11
							12
							13
							14
							15
							16
							17
							18
							19

2. _____

_____

_____

_____

_____

_____

_____

_____

_____

_____

_____

_____

APPENDIX EXERCISES

Exercise 5Apx-1A

Straight-Line Depreciation

Year	Depreciable Cost	x	Rate	=	Depreciation Expense	Accumulated Depreciation End of Year	Book Value End of Year
——	——		——		——	——	——
——	——		——		——	——	——
——	——		——		——	——	——
——	——		——		——	——	——

Exercise 5Apx-2A

Sum-of-the-Years'-Digits

Year	Depreciable Cost	x	Rate	=	Depreciation Expense	Accumulated Depreciation End of Year	Book Value End of Year
——	——		——		——	——	——
——	——		——		——	——	——
——	——		——		——	——	——
——	——		——		——	——	——

Exercise 5Apx-3A

Double-Declining-Balance Method

Year	Book Value Beginning of Year	x	Rate	=	Depreciation Expense	Accumulated Depreciation End of Year	Book Value End of Year
——	——		——		——	——	——
——	——		——		——	——	——
——	——		——		——	——	——
——	——		——		——	——	——

Exercise 5Apx-4A

Modified Accelerated Cost Recovery System

Year	Cost	x	Rate	=	Depreciation Expense	Accumulated Depreciation End of Year	Book Value End of Year
____	____		____		____	____	____
____	____		____		____	____	____
____	____		____		____	____	____
____	____		____		____	____	____
____	____		____		____	____	____
____	____		____		____	____	____

Exercise 5Apx-1B

Straight-Line Depreciation

Year	Depreciable Cost	x	Rate	=	Depreciation Expense	Accumulated Depreciation End of Year	Book Value End of Year
____	____		____		____	____	____
____	____		____		____	____	____
____	____		____		____	____	____
____	____		____		____	____	____
____	____		____		____	____	____

Exercise 5Apx-2B

Sum-of-the-Years'-Digits

Year	Depreciable Cost	x	Rate	=	Depreciation Expense	Accumulated Depreciation End of Year	Book Value End of Year
____	____		____		____	____	____
____	____		____		____	____	____
____	____		____		____	____	____
____	____		____		____	____	____
____	____		____		____	____	____

Exercise 5Apx-3B

Double-Declining-Balance Method

Year	Book Value Beginning of Year	x	Rate	=	Depreciation Expense	Accumulated Depreciation End of Year	Book Value End of Year
____	____		____		____	____	____
____	____		____		____	____	____
____	____		____		____	____	____
____	____		____		____	____	____
____	____		____		____	____	____

Exercise 5Apx-4B

Modified Accelerated Cost Recovery System

Year	Cost	x	Rate	=	Depreciation Expense	Accumulated Depreciation End of Year	Book Value End of Year
____	____		____		____	____	____
____	____		____		____	____	____
____	____		____		____	____	____
____	____		____		____	____	____
____	____		____		____	____	____
____	____		____		____	____	____

Exercise 6-1A

Exercise 6-2A

Exercise 6-3A

Exercise 6-4A

GENERAL JOURNAL

PAGE 1

	DATE	DESCRIPTION	POST. REF.	DEBIT	CREDIT	
1						1
2						2
3						3
4						4
5						5
6						6
7						7
8						8
9						9
10						10
11						11
12						12
13						13
14						14
15						15
16						16
17						17
18						18
19						19
20						20
21						21
22						22
23						23

Advising fees
3793 | 3793
Ø

Rent
500 | 500
Ø

Wages
800 | 800
Ø

Supply
120 | 120
Ø

Adv.
80 | 80
Ø

Phone
58 | 58
Ø

Exercise 6-4A (Concluded)

Electricity

44	44
0	

Gas & oil

38	38
0	

Misc

33	33
0	

Capital

800	4000
	1990
	5190 Bal

Ins Exp

30	30
0	

Dep Exp

100	100
0	

Drawing

800	800
0	

Income Summary

1803	3793
1990	1990 Bal
0	

Exercise 6-5A

GENERAL JOURNAL

PAGE 2

	DATE		DESCRIPTION	POST. REF.	DEBIT	CREDIT	
1			Closing Entry				1
2			Advising fees	401	3 793 00		2
3			Inc Summary			3 793 00	3
4							4
5			Inc Summary				5
6			Wages				6
7			Adv				7
8			Rent				8
9			Suppl				9
10			Phone				10
11			Elect.				11
12			Ins				12
13			G&O				13
14			Dep Exp				14
15			Misc				15
16							16
17		31	Inc Summary		1 990 00		17
18			Capital			1 990 00	18
19							19
20		31	Capital		800 00		20
21			Drawing			800 00	21
22							22
23							23
24							24
25							25
26							26
27							27
28							28
29							29
30							30
31							31
32							32
33							33
34							34
35							35
36							36

Exercise 6-5A (Concluded)

Accum. Depr.—Delivery Equip. 185.1		Wages Payable 219	
	Bal. 100		Bal. 200

Saburo Goto, Capital 311		Saburo Goto, Drawing 312	
	Bal. 4,000	Bal. 800	

Income Summary 313		Delivery Fees 401	
			Bal. 2,200

Wages Expense 511		Advertising Expense 512	
Bal. 1,800		Bal. 80	

Rent Expense 521		Supplies Expense 523	
Bal. 500		Bal. 120	

Telephone Expense 525		Electricity Expense 533	
Bal. 58		Bal. 44	

Insurance Expense 535		Gas & Oil Expense 538	
Bal. 30		Bal. 38	

Depr. Exp.—Delivery Equip. 541		Miscellaneous Expense 549	
Bal. 100		Bal. 33	

Problem 6-6A

1.

2.

Problem 6-6A (Concluded)

3.

Problem 6-7A

_____

_____

_____

Problem 6-8A

1.

GENERAL JOURNAL   PAGE 10

	DATE		DESCRIPTION	POST. REF.	DEBIT	CREDIT	
1							1
2							2
3							3
4							4
5							5
6							6
7							7
8							8
9							9
10							10
11							11
12							12
13							13
14							14
15							15
16							16
17							17
18							18

Problem 6-8A (Continued)

2.

GENERAL JOURNAL

PAGE 11

	DATE	DESCRIPTION	POST. REF.	DEBIT	CREDIT	
1						1
2						2
3						3
4						4
5						5
6						6
7						7
8						8
9						9
10						10
11						11
12						12
13						13
14						14
15						15
16						16
17						17
18						18
19						19
20						20
21						21
22						22
23						23

GENERAL LEDGER

ACCOUNT Cash

ACCOUNT NO. 101

DATE	ITEM	POST. REF.	DEBIT	CREDIT	BALANCE DEBIT	BALANCE CREDIT
20-- Jan. 31	Balance	✓			3 0 8 0 00	

Problem 6-8A (Continued)

ACCOUNT   Accounts Receivable   ACCOUNT NO. 122

DATE		ITEM	POST. REF.	DEBIT	CREDIT	BALANCE DEBIT	BALANCE CREDIT
20-- Jan.	31	Balance	✓			1 2 0 0 00	

ACCOUNT   Supplies   ACCOUNT NO. 141

DATE		ITEM	POST. REF.	DEBIT	CREDIT	BALANCE DEBIT	BALANCE CREDIT
20-- Jan.	31	Balance	✓			8 0 0 00	

ACCOUNT   Prepaid Insurance   ACCOUNT NO. 145

DATE		ITEM	POST. REF.	DEBIT	CREDIT	BALANCE DEBIT	BALANCE CREDIT
20-- Jan.	31	Balance	✓			9 0 0 00	

ACCOUNT   Delivery Equipment   ACCOUNT NO. 185

DATE		ITEM	POST. REF.	DEBIT	CREDIT	BALANCE DEBIT	BALANCE CREDIT
20-- Jan.	31	Balance	✓			3 0 0 0 00	

ACCOUNT   Accumulated Depreciation—Delivery Equipment   ACCOUNT NO. 185.1

DATE		ITEM	POST. REF.	DEBIT	CREDIT	BALANCE DEBIT	BALANCE CREDIT

Problem 6-8A(Continued)

ACCOUNT   Accounts Payable   ACCOUNT NO. 202

DATE	ITEM	POST. REF.	DEBIT	CREDIT	BALANCE DEBIT	BALANCE CREDIT
20-- Jan. 31	Balance	✓				1 1 0 0 00

ACCOUNT   Wages Payable   ACCOUNT NO. 219

DATE	ITEM	POST. REF.	DEBIT	CREDIT	BALANCE DEBIT	BALANCE CREDIT

ACCOUNT   Monte Eli, Capital   ACCOUNT NO. 311

DATE	ITEM	POST. REF.	DEBIT	CREDIT	BALANCE DEBIT	BALANCE CREDIT
20-- Jan. 31	Balance	✓				7 0 0 0 00

ACCOUNT   Monte Eli, Drawing   ACCOUNT NO. 312

DATE	ITEM	POST. REF.	DEBIT	CREDIT	BALANCE DEBIT	BALANCE CREDIT
20-- Jan. 31	Balance	✓			1 0 0 0 00	

ACCOUNT   Income Summary   ACCOUNT NO. 313

DATE	ITEM	POST. REF.	DEBIT	CREDIT	BALANCE DEBIT	BALANCE CREDIT

Problem 6-8A (Continued)

ACCOUNT Repair Fees   ACCOUNT NO. 401

DATE		ITEM	POST. REF.	DEBIT	CREDIT	BALANCE DEBIT	BALANCE CREDIT
20-- Jan.	31	Balance	✓				4 2 3 0 00

ACCOUNT Wages Expense   ACCOUNT NO. 511

DATE		ITEM	POST. REF.	DEBIT	CREDIT	BALANCE DEBIT	BALANCE CREDIT
20-- Jan.	31	Balance	✓			1 6 5 0 00	

ACCOUNT Advertising Expense   ACCOUNT NO. 512

DATE		ITEM	POST. REF.	DEBIT	CREDIT	BALANCE DEBIT	BALANCE CREDIT
20-- Jan.	31	Balance	✓			1 7 0 00	

ACCOUNT Rent Expense   ACCOUNT NO. 521

DATE		ITEM	POST. REF.	DEBIT	CREDIT	BALANCE DEBIT	BALANCE CREDIT
20-- Jan.	31	Balance	✓			4 2 0 00	

ACCOUNT Supplies Expense   ACCOUNT NO. 523

DATE		ITEM	POST. REF.	DEBIT	CREDIT	BALANCE DEBIT	BALANCE CREDIT

Problem 6-8A (Continued)

ACCOUNT I Telephone Expense   ACCOUNT NO. 525

DATE		ITEM	POST. REF.	DEBIT	CREDIT	BALANCE	
						DEBIT	CREDIT
20-- Jan.	31	Balance	✓			4 9 00	

ACCOUNT Insurance Expense   ACCOUNT NO. 535

DATE		ITEM	POST. REF.	DEBIT	CREDIT	BALANCE	
						DEBIT	CREDIT

ACCOUNT Gas and Oil Expense   ACCOUNT NO. 538

DATE		ITEM	POST. REF.	DEBIT	CREDIT	BALANCE	
						DEBIT	CREDIT
20-- Jan.	31	Balance	✓			3 3 00	

ACCOUNT Depreciation Expense—Delivery Equipment   ACCOUNT NO. 541

DATE		ITEM	POST. REF.	DEBIT	CREDIT	BALANCE	
						DEBIT	CREDIT

ACCOUNT Miscellaneous Expense   ACCOUNT NO. 549

DATE		ITEM	POST. REF.	DEBIT	CREDIT	BALANCE	
						DEBIT	CREDIT
20-- Jan.	31	Balance	✓			2 8 00	

Problem 6-8A (Concluded)

3.

_____

_____

_____

ACCOUNT	ACCT. NO.	DEBIT BALANCE	CREDIT BALANCE

Exercise 6-1B

Exercise 6-2B

Mastery Problem

Mastery Problem (Continued)

Mastery Problem (Concluded)

GENERAL JOURNAL

	DATE		DESCRIPTION	POST. REF.	DEBIT	CREDIT	
1							1
2							2
3							3
4							4
5							5
6							6
7							7
8							8
9							9
10							10
11							11
12							12
13							13
14							14
15							15
16							16
17							17
18							18
19							19
20							20
21							21
22							22
23							23
24							24
25							25
26							26
27							27
28							28
29							29
30							30
31							31
32							32
33							33
34							34
35							35
36							36

Challenge Problem

Challenge Problem (Concluded)

Exercise 6Apx-1A

a. _____

b. _____

c. _____

d. _____

e. _____

f. _____

g. _____

h. _____

i. _____

j. _____

k. _____

Problem 6Apx-2A

Exercise 6Apx-1B

a. _____   g. _____

b. _____   h. _____

c. _____   i. _____

d. _____   j. _____

e. _____   k. _____

f. _____

Problem 6Apx-2B

Comprehensive Problem 1, Period 2: The Accounting Cycle

GENERAL JOURNAL

	DATE		DESCRIPTION	POST. REF.	DEBIT	CREDIT	
1							1
2							2
3							3
4							4
5							5
6							6
7							7
8							8
9							9
10							10
11							11
12							12
13							13
14							14
15							15
16							16
17							17
18							18
19							19
20							20
21							21
22							22
23							23
24							24
25							25
26							26
27							27
28							28
29							29
30							30
31							31
32							32
33							33
34							34
35							35
36							36

Comprehensive Problem 1, Period 2 (Continued)

GENERAL JOURNAL

	DATE		DESCRIPTION	POST. REF.	DEBIT	CREDIT	
1							1
2							2
3							3
4							4
5							5
6							6
7							7
8							8
9							9
10							10
11							11
12							12
13							13
14							14
15							15
16							16
17							17
18							18
19							19
20							20
21							21
22							22
23							23
24							24
25							25
26							26
27							27
28							28
29							29
30							30
31							31
32							32
33							33
34							34
35							35
36							36
37							37
38							38
39							39
40							40
41							41
42							42

Comprehensive Problem 1, Period 2 (Continued)

GENERAL JOURNAL   PAGE 7

	DATE		DESCRIPTION	POST. REF.	DEBIT	CREDIT	
1							1
2							2
3							3
4							4
5							5
6							6
7							7
8							8
9							9
10							10
11							11
12							12
13							13
14							14
15							15
16							16
17							17
18							18
19							19
20							20
21							21
22							22
23							23
24							24
25							25
26							26
27							27
28							28
29							29
30							30
31							31
32							32
33							33
34							34

Comprehensive Problem 1, Period 2 (Continued)

2., 9., and 11.

GENERAL LEDGER

ACCOUNT Cash   ACCOUNT NO.   101

DATE		ITEM	POST. REF.	DEBIT	CREDIT	BALANCE	
						DEBIT	CREDIT
20— Apr.	30	Balance	✓			130 6 5 0 00	

ACCOUNT Accounts Receivable   ACCOUNT NO.   122

DATE	ITEM	POST. REF.	DEBIT	CREDIT	BALANCE	
					DEBIT	CREDIT

Comprehensive Problem 1, Period 2 (Continued)

ACCOUNT **Office Supplies**   ACCOUNT NO. 142

DATE		ITEM	POST. REF.	DEBIT	CREDIT	BALANCE DEBIT	BALANCE CREDIT
20— Apr.	30	Balance	✔			1 0 0 00	

ACCOUNT **Food Supplies**   ACCOUNT NO. 144

DATE		ITEM	POST. REF.	DEBIT	CREDIT	BALANCE DEBIT	BALANCE CREDIT
20— Apr.	30	Balance	✔			8 0 0 0 00	

ACCOUNT **Prepaid Insurance**   ACCOUNT NO. 145

DATE		ITEM	POST. REF.	DEBIT	CREDIT	BALANCE DEBIT	BALANCE CREDIT
20— Apr.	30	Balance	✔			7 5 0 0 00	

ACCOUNT **Prepaid Subscriptions**   ACCOUNT NO. 146

DATE	ITEM	POST. REF.	DEBIT	CREDIT	BALANCE DEBIT	BALANCE CREDIT

Comprehensive Problem 1, Period 2 (Continued)

ACCOUNT Land   ACCOUNT NO. 161

DATE	ITEM	POST. REF.	DEBIT	CREDIT	BALANCE	
					DEBIT	CREDIT

ACCOUNT Building   ACCOUNT NO. 171

DATE	ITEM	POST. REF.	DEBIT	CREDIT	BALANCE	
					DEBIT	CREDIT

ACCOUNT Accumulated Depreciation—Buildings   ACCOUNT NO. 171.1

DATE	ITEM	POST. REF.	DEBIT	CREDIT	BALANCE	
					DEBIT	CREDIT

ACCOUNT Fishing Boats   ACCOUNT NO. 181

DATE		ITEM	POST. REF.	DEBIT	CREDIT	BALANCE	
						DEBIT	CREDIT
20— Apr.	30	Balance	✔			60 0 0 0 00	

Comprehensive Problem 1, Period 2 (Continued)

ACCOUNT Accumulated Depreciation—Fishing Boats   ACCOUNT NO.   181.1

DATE		ITEM	POST. REF.	DEBIT	CREDIT	BALANCE DEBIT	BALANCE CREDIT
20—Apr.	30	Balance	✓				1 0 0 0 00

ACCOUNT Surround Sound System   ACCOUNT NO.   182

DATE	ITEM	POST. REF.	DEBIT	CREDIT	BALANCE DEBIT	BALANCE CREDIT

ACCOUNT Accumulated Depreciation—Surround Sound System   ACCOUNT NO.   182.1

DATE	ITEM	POST. REF.	DEBIT	CREDIT	BALANCE DEBIT	BALANCE CREDIT

ACCOUNT Big Screen TV   ACCOUNT NO.   183

DATE	ITEM	POST. REF.	DEBIT	CREDIT	BALANCE DEBIT	BALANCE CREDIT

ACCOUNT Accumulated Depreciation—Big Screen TV   ACCOUNT NO.   183.1

DATE	ITEM	POST. REF.	DEBIT	CREDIT	BALANCE DEBIT	BALANCE CREDIT

Comprehensive Problem 1, Period 2 (Continued)

ACCOUNT Accounts Payable   ACCOUNT NO. 202

DATE		ITEM	POST. REF.	DEBIT	CREDIT	BALANCE DEBIT	BALANCE CREDIT
20— Apr.	30	Balance	✓				66 5 0 0 00

ACCOUNT Wages Payable   ACCOUNT NO. 219

DATE		ITEM	POST. REF.	DEBIT	CREDIT	BALANCE DEBIT	BALANCE CREDIT
20— Apr.	30	Balance	✓				5 0 0 00

ACCOUNT Bob Night, Capital   ACCOUNT NO. 311

DATE		ITEM	POST. REF.	DEBIT	CREDIT	BALANCE DEBIT	BALANCE CREDIT
20— Apr.	30	Balance	✓				138 2 5 0 00

ACCOUNT Bob Night, Drawing   ACCOUNT NO. 312

DATE		ITEM	POST. REF.	DEBIT	CREDIT	BALANCE DEBIT	BALANCE CREDIT

Comprehensive Problem 1, Period 2 (Continued)

ACCOUNT   Income Summary   ACCOUNT NO.   313

DATE	ITEM	POST. REF.	DEBIT	CREDIT	BALANCE DEBIT	BALANCE CREDIT

ACCOUNT   Registration Fees   ACCOUNT NO.   401

DATE	ITEM	POST. REF.	DEBIT	CREDIT	BALANCE DEBIT	BALANCE CREDIT

ACCOUNT   Vending Revenue   ACCOUNT NO.   404

DATE	ITEM	POST. REF.	DEBIT	CREDIT	BALANCE DEBIT	BALANCE CREDIT

ACCOUNT   Wages Expense   ACCOUNT NO.   511

DATE	ITEM	POST. REF.	DEBIT	CREDIT	BALANCE DEBIT	BALANCE CREDIT

Comprehensive Problem 1, Period 2 (Continued)

ACCOUNT Advertising Expense   ACCOUNT NO. 512

DATE	ITEM	POST. REF.	DEBIT	CREDIT	BALANCE DEBIT	BALANCE CREDIT

ACCOUNT Rent Expense   ACCOUNT NO. 521

DATE	ITEM	POST. REF.	DEBIT	CREDIT	BALANCE DEBIT	BALANCE CREDIT

ACCOUNT Office Supplies Expense   ACCOUNT NO. 523

DATE	ITEM	POST. REF.	DEBIT	CREDIT	BALANCE DEBIT	BALANCE CREDIT

ACCOUNT Food Supplies Expense   ACCOUNT NO. 524

DATE	ITEM	POST. REF.	DEBIT	CREDIT	BALANCE DEBIT	BALANCE CREDIT

Comprehensive Problem 1, Period 2 (Continued)

ACCOUNT Telephone Expense   ACCOUNT NO.   525

DATE	ITEM	POST. REF.	DEBIT	CREDIT	BALANCE DEBIT	BALANCE CREDIT

ACCOUNT Utilities Expense   ACCOUNT NO.   533

DATE	ITEM	POST. REF.	DEBIT	CREDIT	BALANCE DEBIT	BALANCE CREDIT

ACCOUNT Insurance Expense   ACCOUNT NO.   535

DATE	ITEM	POST. REF.	DEBIT	CREDIT	BALANCE DEBIT	BALANCE CREDIT

ACCOUNT Postage Expense   ACCOUNT NO.   536

DATE	ITEM	POST. REF.	DEBIT	CREDIT	BALANCE DEBIT	BALANCE CREDIT

Comprehensive Problem 1, Period 2 (Continued)

ACCOUNT Repair Expense   ACCOUNT NO. 537

DATE	ITEM	POST. REF.	DEBIT	CREDIT	BALANCE DEBIT	BALANCE CREDIT

ACCOUNT Depreciation Expense—Buildings   ACCOUNT NO. 540

DATE	ITEM	POST. REF.	DEBIT	CREDIT	BALANCE DEBIT	BALANCE CREDIT

ACCOUNT Depreciation Expense—Surround Sound System   ACCOUNT NO. 541

DATE	ITEM	POST. REF.	DEBIT	CREDIT	BALANCE DEBIT	BALANCE CREDIT

ACCOUNT Depreciation Expense—Fishing Boats   ACCOUNT NO. 542

DATE	ITEM	POST. REF.	DEBIT	CREDIT	BALANCE DEBIT	BALANCE CREDIT

Comprehensive Problem 1, Period 2 (Continued)

ACCOUNT Depreciation Expense—Big Screen TV   ACCOUNT NO.   543

DATE	ITEM	POST. REF.	DEBIT	CREDIT	BALANCE DEBIT	BALANCE CREDIT

ACCOUNT Satellite Programming Expense   ACCOUNT NO.   546

DATE	ITEM	POST. REF.	DEBIT	CREDIT	BALANCE DEBIT	BALANCE CREDIT

ACCOUNT Subscriptions Expense   ACCOUNT NO.   548

DATE	ITEM	POST. REF.	DEBIT	CREDIT	BALANCE DEBIT	BALANCE CREDIT

Comprehensive Problem 1, Period 2 (Continued)
3. and 4.

	ACCOUNT TITLE	TRIAL BALANCE		ADJUSTMENTS	
		DEBIT	CREDIT	DEBIT	CREDIT
1					
2					
3					
4					
5					
6					
7					
8					
9					
10					
11					
12					
13					
14					
15					
16					
17					
18					
19					
20					
21					
22					
23					
24					
25					
26					
27					
28					
29					
30					
31					
32					
33					
34					
35					
36					
37					
38					
39					

Name _____

Comprehensive Problem 1, Period 2 (Continued)

ADJUSTED TRIAL BALANCE		INCOME STATEMENT		BALANCE SHEET		
DEBIT	CREDIT	DEBIT	CREDIT	DEBIT	CREDIT	
						1
						2
						3
						4
						5
						6
						7
						8
						9
						10
						11
						12
						13
						14
						15
						16
						17
						18
						19
						20
						21
						22
						23
						24
						25
						26
						27
						28
						29
						30
						31
						32
						33
						34
						35
						36
						37
						38
						39

Comprehensive Problem 1, Period 2 (Continued)

5.

6.

Comprehensive Problem 1, Period 2 (Continued)

7.

Comprehensive Problem 1, Period 2 (Continued)

8.

	DATE		DESCRIPTION	POST. REF.	DEBIT	CREDIT	
1							1
2							2
3							3
4							4
5							5
6							6
7							7
8							8
9							9
10							10
11							11
12							12
13							13
14							14
15							15
16							16
17							17
18							18
19							19
20							20
21							21
22							22
23							23
24							24
25							25
26							26
27							27
28							28
29							29
30							30
31							31
32							32
33							33
34							34
35							35

Comprehensive Problem 1, Period 2 (Continued)
10.

GENERAL JOURNAL

	DATE	DESCRIPTION	POST. REF.	DEBIT	CREDIT	
1						1
2						2
3						3
4						4
5						5
6						6
7						7
8						8
9						9
10						10
11						11
12						12
13						13
14						14
15						15
16						16
17						17
18						18
19						19
20						20
21						21
22						22
23						23
24						24
25						25
26						26
27						27
28						28
29						29
30						30
31						31
32						32
33						33
34						34
35						35

Comprehensive Problem 1, Period 2 (Concluded)

12.

ACCOUNT	ACCT. NO.	DEBIT BALANCE	CREDIT BALANCE

Exercise 7-1A

1. _____   5. _____
2. _____   6. _____
3. _____   7. _____
4. _____

Exercise 7-2A

WIZARD BANK 3711 Buena Vista Dr. Orlando, FL 32811-1314	**DEPOSIT TICKET**	63-1209 631

CURRENCY		
COIN		
C H E C K S		
TOTAL FROM OTHER SIDE		
SUBTOTAL		
LESS CASH RECEIVED		
NET DEPOSIT		

Date_____ 20____

CHECKS AND OTHER ITEMS ARE RECEIVED FOR DEPOSIT SUBJECT TO THE TERMS AND CONDITIONS OF THIS FINANCIAL INSTITUTION'S ACCOUNT AGREEMENT.

SIGN HERE ONLY IF CASH RECEIVED FROM DEPOSIT

⑆063112094⑆ 0001632475⑈

Exercise 7-3A

No. 1		
DATE _____ 20____		
TO _____		
FOR _____		
ACCT. _____		

	DOLLARS	CENTS
BAL BRO'T FOR'D		
AMT. DEPOSITED		
TOTAL		
AMT. THIS CHECK		
BAL CAR'D FOR'D		

No. 1   63-1209 / 631

_____ 20_____

PAY
TO THE
ORDER OF _____ $ _____

_____ Dollars

WIZARD BANK   FOR CLASSROOM USE ONLY
3711 Buena Vista Dr.
Orlando, FL 32811-1314

MEMO_____   BY _____

⑆063112094⑆ 0001632475⑈

Exercise 7-4A

	Ending Bank Balance	Ending Check-book Balance
1.	_____	_____
2.	_____	_____
3.	_____	_____
4.	_____	_____
5.	_____	_____
6.	_____	_____
7.	_____	_____

Exercise 7-5A

GENERAL JOURNAL

PAGE _____

	DATE	DESCRIPTION	POST. REF.	DEBIT	CREDIT	
1						1
2						2
3						3
4						4
5						5
6						6
7						7
8						8
9						9
10						10
11						11
12						12
13						13
14						14
15						15
16						16
17						17
18						18
19						19
20						20
21						21

Exercise 7-6A

GENERAL JOURNAL

PAGE

	DATE		DESCRIPTION	POST. REF.	DEBIT	CREDIT	
1							1
2							2
3							3
4							4
5							5
6							6
7							7
8							8
9							9
10							10
11							11
12							12
13							13
14							14
15							15
16							16
17							17
18							18
19							19
20							20
21							21
22							22
23							23
24							24
25							25
26							26
27							27
28							28
29							29
30							30
31							31
32							32
33							33
34							34
35							35
36							36

Exercise 7-7A

GENERAL JOURNAL

PAGE

	DATE		DESCRIPTION	POST. REF.	DEBIT	CREDIT	
1	2007 Apr	2	Cash		266 50		1
2			Cash Short and Over		2 00		2
3			Sales			268 60	3
4			Sale 4/2/07				4
5							5
6		9	Cash		233 50		6
7			Cash Short and Over		4 25		7
8			Sales			237 75	8
9			Sale 4/9				9
10							10
11		16	Cash		311 00		11
12			Cash Short and Over			1 75	12
13			Sales			309 75	13
14			Sale 4/16				14
15							15
16							16
17							17
18							18
19							19
20							20
21							21
22							22
23							23
24							24
25							25
26							26
27							27
28							28
29							29
30							30
31							31
32							32
33							33
34							34
35							35
36							36

Problem 7-8A

1.

Violette Enterprise
Bank Rec.
Oct 31, 2007

Bank Statement Bal. 10/31								#	4	2 3	5 00
Add:											
Deposits in Transit			1 7 5 00							
10/29			3 3 4 00			5 0 9 00			
10/31						4 7 4 4 00			
Deduct:											
Outstanding checks										
#1764			4 7 00							
#1767			1 4 6 00							
#1781			3 6 9 00			5 6 2 00			
Adjusted Bank Balance						# 4 1 8 2 00			
Bal per Book Oct 31										
Add:											
Error ck#1754		#	1 0 0 00							
Deduct:											
unrecorded ATM			1 8 0 00							
Bank svc charge			4 3 00							
NSF check			3 7 0 00			5 9 3 00			
Adjusted Book Bal.						# 4 1 8 2 00			

Problem 7-8A (Concluded)
2.

GENERAL JOURNAL

PAGE

DATE			DESCRIPTION	POST. REF.	DEBIT	CREDIT	
2001 Oct	31		Cash		1000		1
			Accts Payable			1000	2
			Error in ck #1754				3
							4
	31		Vinlette Drawing		18000		5
			Cash			18000	6
			unrecorded ATM				7
							8
	31		Miscellaneous Exp.		4300		9
			Cash			4300	10
			Record svc fee Out.				11
							12
	31		A/R		37000		13
			Cash			37000	14
			NSF check				15

Problem 7-9A

1.

2.

GENERAL JOURNAL

PAGE

	DATE		DESCRIPTION	POST. REF.	DEBIT	CREDIT	
1							1
2							2
3							3
4							4
5							5
6							6
7							7
8							8
9							9
10							10

Problem 7-10A

1. and 3.

GENERAL JOURNAL

PAGE

	DATE		DESCRIPTION	POST. REF.	DEBIT	CREDIT	
1	2007 May	1	Petty Cash		1 5 0 00		1
2			Cash			1 5 0 00	2
3			To establish petty cash fund				3
4							4
5			OFc Supplies		1 1 00		5
6			Postage Exp.		3 50		6
7			Char. Contri.		4 0 00		7
8			Telephone		5 00		8
9			T & E		2 8 00		9
10			Misc Exp.		2 2 00		10
11			J Adams Drawing		2 5 00		11
12			Cash			1 3 8 00	12
13			To replenish Petty cash fund				13

Problem 7-10A (Concluded)
2. and 3.

PETTY CASH PAYMENTS FOR MONTH OF May 20--07   PAGE

DAY	DESCRIPTION	VOU. NO.	TOTAL AMOUNT	OFFICE SUPPLIES	POSTAGE EXPENSE	CHARIT. CONTRIB. EXPENSE	TELEPHONE EXPENSE	TRAVEL & ENTER. EXPENSE	MISC. EXPENSE	ACCOUNT	AMOUNT
1	Received in funds $500.00										
1	Postage		3 50		3 50						
3	Office Supplies		11 00	11 00							
5	Auto repair		22 00						22 00		
7	J Adams, Drawing		25 00							J Adams, Drawing	25 00
11			10 00								
			28 00								

Problem 7-11A

1.

GENERAL JOURNAL

PAGE 8

DATE	DESCRIPTION	POST. REF.	DEBIT	CREDIT	
1					1
2					2
3					3
4					4
5					5
6					6
7					7
8					8
9					9
10					10
11					11
12					12
13					13
14					14
15					15
16					16
17					17
18					18
19					19

2.

ACCOUNT

ACCOUNT NO.

DATE	ITEM	POST. REF.	DEBIT	CREDIT	BALANCE	
					DEBIT	CREDIT

3. The balance represents:

_____

Problem 7-8B

1.

Problem 7-8B (Concluded)

2.

GENERAL JOURNAL

PAGE

	DATE	DESCRIPTION	POST. REF.	DEBIT	CREDIT	
1						1
2						2
3						3
4						4
5						5
6						6
7						7
8						8
9						9
10						10
11						11
12						12
13						13
14						14
15						15

Mastery Problem

1.

PETTY CASH PAYMENTS FOR MONTH OF _____ 20--   PAGE ____

DAY	DESCRIPTION	VOU. NO.	TOTAL AMOUNT	TRUCK EXPENSE	POSTAGE EXPENSE	CHARIT. CONTRIB. EXPENSE	TELEPHONE EXPENSE	ADVERT. EXPENSE.	MISC. EXPENSE	ACCOUNT	AMOUNT	
												1
												2
												3
												4
												5
												6
												7
												8
												9
												10
												11
												12
												13
												14
												15
												16
												17
												18
												19
												20
												21
												22

DISTRIBUTION OF PAYMENTS

Mastery Problem (Continued)
2. and 3.

GENERAL JOURNAL

PAGE

	DATE		DESCRIPTION	POST. REF.	DEBIT	CREDIT	
1							1
2							2
3							3
4							4
5							5
6							6
7							7
8							8
9							9
10							10
11							11
12							12
13							13
14							14
15							15
16							16
17							17
18							18
19							19
20							20
21							21
22							22
23							23
24							24
25							25
26							26
27							27
28							28
29							29
30							30
31							31
32							32
33							33
34							34
35							35

Mastery Problem (Concluded)

GENERAL JOURNAL

	DATE	DESCRIPTION	POST. REF.	DEBIT	CREDIT	
1						1
2						2
3						3
4						4
5						5
6						6
7						7
8						8
9						9
10						10
11						11
12						12
13						13
14						14

3.

Challenge Problem

1. Panera Bakery

GENERAL JOURNAL   PAGE

	DATE	DESCRIPTION	POST. REF.	DEBIT	CREDIT	
1						1
2						2
3						3
4						4
5						5
6						6
7						7
8						8
9						9
10						10
11						11
12						12
13						13
14						14
15						15
16						16
17						17
18						18
19						19
20						20
21						21
22						22
23						23
24						24
25						25
26						26
27						27
28						28
29						29

Challenge Problem (Concluded)

2. Lawrence Bank

GENERAL JOURNAL   PAGE _____

	DATE		DESCRIPTION	POST. REF.	DEBIT	CREDIT	
1							1
2							2
3							3
4							4
5							5
6							6
7							7
8							8
9							9
10							10
11							11
12							12
13							13
14							14
15							15
16							16
17							17
18							18
19							19
20							20
21							21
22							22
23							23
24							24
25							25
26							26
27							27
28							28
29							29

Exercise 8-1A

a. _____ regular hours × $10.00 per hour   _____

b. _____ overtime hours × $15.00 per hour   _____

c. Total gross wages   _____

d. Federal income tax withholding
   (from tax tables in Figure 8-4)   _____

e. Social security withholding at 6.2%   _____

f. Medicare withholding at 1.45%   _____

g. Total withholding   _____

h. Net pay   _____

Exercise 8-2A

M T W Th F Sun = 47   15 × 1.5 = 22.50
8   8 8   8   10   5   40 × 15 600.
40 15   2 × 22.50 = 45
2   5 × 30 = 150
5 30 $ 795

Exercise 8-3A

22000   1200   23200   87,000   0   1200

_____

_____

_____

_____

_____

_____

_____

Exercise 8-4A

	Marital Status	Total Weekly Earnings	Number of Allowances	Amount of Withholding
a.	S	$327.90	2	_____
b.	S	410.00	1	_____
c.	M	438.16	5	_____
d.	S	518.25	0	_____
e.	M	603.98	6	_____

Exercise 8-5A

Cumulative Pay Before Current Weekly Payroll	Current Gross Pay	Year-to-Date Earnings	Social Security Max.	Amount over Max. Soc. Sec.	Amount Subject to Soc. Sec	Social Sec. Tax Withheld	Medicare Tax Withheld
$22,000	$1,200	23,200	$87,000	∅	1200	74.40	17.40
54,000	4,200	58,200	87,000	∅	4200	260.40	60.90
84,400	3,925	88,325	87,000	1,325	2600	161.20	56.91
86,400	4,600	91,000	87,000	4,000	600	37.20	66.70

Exercise 8-6A

GENERAL JOURNAL   PAGE

	DATE	DESCRIPTION	POST. REF.	DEBIT	CREDIT	
1						1
2						2
3						3
4						4
5						5
6						6
7						7
8						8
9						9

Exercise 8-7A

GENERAL JOURNAL   PAGE

	DATE	DESCRIPTION	POST. REF.	DEBIT	CREDIT	
1	2001 Apr 15	Wages & Salaries Exp		6 242 00		1
2		Employee FIT			593 00	2
3		SS pay			387 00	3
4		Medicare			90 51	4
5		Per Pay			90 00	5
6		Health Ins			225 00	6
7		United Way Contri			100 00	7
8		Cash			4 756 49	8
9		Payroll for week ended Apr 15				9

Problem 8-8A

1.

_____

_____

_____

_____

_____

_____

_____

_____

_____

_____

_____

_____

_____

_____

_____

_____

_____

_____

2.

GENERAL JOURNAL   PAGE

	DATE		DESCRIPTION	POST. REF.	DEBIT	CREDIT	
1							1
2							2
3							3
4							4
5							5
6							6
7							7
8							8
9							9
10							10
11							11
12							12
13							13
14							14
15							15

Problem 8-9A

1.

PAYROLL REGISTER

	NAME	NO. ALLOW.	MARIT. STATUS	EARNINGS				CUMULATIVE TOTAL	TAXABLE EARNINGS		
				REGULAR		OVERTIME	TOTAL		UNEMPLOY. COMP.	SOCIAL SECURITY	
1											
2											
3											
4											
5											
6											
7											
8											
9											
10											
11											
12											
13											
14											

Problem 8-9A (Concluded)

FOR PERIOD ENDED   20--

					DEDUCTIONS 6.2 1.45 100					
FEDERAL INCOME TAX	SOCIAL SECURITY TAX	MEDICARE TAX	CITY TAX	HEALTH INSUR.	OTHER		TOTAL	NET PAY	CK. NO.	
										1
										2
										3
										4
										5
										6
										7
										8
										9
										10
										11
										12
										13
										14

2.

GENERAL JOURNAL   PAGE

	DATE	DESCRIPTION	POST. REF.	DEBIT	CREDIT	
1						1
2						2
3						3
4						4
5						5
6						6
7						7
8						8
9						9
10						10
11						11
12						12
13						13
14						14

Problem 8-10A

EMPLOYEE EARNINGS RECORD

20 -- PERIOD ENDED	EARNINGS				TAXABLE EARNINGS		DEDUCTIONS	
	REGULAR	OVERTIME	TOTAL	CUMULATIVE TOTAL	UNEMPLOY. COMP.	SOCIAL SECURITY	FEDERAL INCOME TAX	SOCIAL SECURITY TAX

GENDER		DEPARTMENT	OCCUPATION	SOCIAL SECURITY NO.	MARITAL STATUS	ALLOW-ANCES
M	F					

Problem 8-10B (Concluded)

FOR PERIOD ENDED 20--

			DEDUCTIONS					
MEDICARE TAX	CITY TAX	HEALTH INSURANCE	OTHER		TOTAL	CK. NO.	AMOUNT	
								1
								2
								3
								4
								5
PAY RATE	DATE OF BIRTH	DATE HIRED	NAME/ADDRESS				EMP NO.	6
								7

Mastery Problem

1.

PAYROLL REGISTER

	NAME	NO. ALLOW.	MARIT. STATUS	EARNINGS				CUMULATIVE TOTAL	TAXABLE EARNINGS		
				REGULAR		OVERTIME	TOTAL		UNEMPLOY. COMP.	SOCIAL SECURITY	
1											
2											
3											
4											
5											
6											
7											
8											
9											
10											
11											
12											
13											
14											

3.

EMPLOYEE EARNINGS RECORD

20 -- PERIOD ENDED	EARNINGS				CUMULATIVE TOTAL	TAXABLE EARNINGS		FEDERAL INCOME TAX
	REGULAR		OVERTIME	TOTAL		UNEMPLOY. COMP.	SOCIAL SECURITY	
11/4	330 00		33 00	363 00	6,145 50	363 00	363 00	1 00
11/11	440 00		49 50	489 50	6,635 00	489 50	489 50	13 00
11/18								
11/25								

GENDER		DEPARTMENT	OCCUPATION	SOCIAL SECURITY NO.	MARITAL STATUS
M	F				

Mastery Problem (Continued)

FOR PERIOD ENDED   20--

			DEDUCTIONS						
FEDERAL INCOME TAX	SOCIAL SECURITY TAX	MEDICARE TAX	STATE INCOME TAX	HEALTH INSURANCE	CREDIT UNION	TOTAL	NET PAY	CK. NO.	
									1
									2
									3
									4
									5
									6
									7
									8
									9
									10
									11
									12
									13
									14

FOR PERIOD ENDED   20--

			DEDUCTIONS					NET PAY	
SOCIAL SECURITY TAX	MEDICARE TAX	STATE INCOME TAX	HEALTH INSURANCE	CREDIT UNION	TOTAL	CK. NO.	AMOUNT		
22 51	5 26	12 71		72 60	114 08	121	248 92		1
30 35	7 10	17 13		97 90	165 48	229	324 02		2
									3
									4
									5

ALLOWANCES	PAY RATE	DATE OF BIRTH	DATE HIRED	NAME/ADDRESS	EMP. NO.
					6
					7

Mastery Problem (Concluded)

2.

GENERAL JOURNAL

PAGE

	DATE	DESCRIPTION	POST. REF.	DEBIT	CREDIT	
1						1
2						2
3						3
4						4
5						5
6						6
7						7
8						8
9						9
10						10
11						11
12						12
13						13
14						14
15						15
16						16
17						17
18						18
19						19
20						20
21						21
22						22
23						23
24						24
25						25
26						26
27						27
28						28
29						29
30						30
31						31
32						32
33						33
34						34
35						35

Challenge Problem

1.

GENERAL JOURNAL

PAGE

	DATE		DESCRIPTION	POST. REF.	DEBIT	CREDIT	
1							1
2							2
3							3
4							4
5							5
6							6
7							7
8							8
9							9
10							10

2.

Exercise 9-1A

1.

_____

_____

_____

_____

_____

2.

		GENERAL JOURNAL			PAGE

	DATE	DESCRIPTION	POST. REF.	DEBIT	CREDIT	
1						1
2						2
3						3
4						4
5						5
6						6
7						7

Exercise 9-2A

Futa 710 × .8% = $5.68

Suta 710 × 5.4%   38.34

Soc Sec 4000 × 6.2% $248.

Medicare 4000 × 1.45%   58

		GENERAL JOURNAL			PAGE

	DATE	DESCRIPTION	POST. REF.	DEBIT	CREDIT	
1	1007 Mar 12	Payroll Tax Expense		350 02		1
2		Futa			5 68	2
3		Suta			38 34	3
4		Soc Sec			248 00	4
5		Medicare Tax Pay			58 00	5
6		record Payroll Taxes				6
7						7

Exercise 9-3A

		Taxable Earnings	
Name	**Total Earnings**	**Unemploy. Comp.**	**Social Security**
Burgos			
Ellis			
Lewis			
Mason			
Yates			
Zielke			
Total			

GENERAL JOURNAL

PAGE

	DATE	DESCRIPTION	POST. REF.	DEBIT	CREDIT	
1						1
2						2
3						3
4						4
5						5
6						6
7						7

Exercise 9-4A

Exercise 9-5A

GENERAL JOURNAL
PAGE

	DATE	DESCRIPTION	POST. REF.	DEBIT	CREDIT	
1	2007 4 15	Employee Inc. Pay		2275		1
2		Soc. Sec Pay		3750		2
3		Medicare Pay		875		3
4		Cash			690000	4
5		To record 941				5
6						6
7	30	Futa Tax Pay		20000		7
8		Cash			20000	8
9		Futa Payment				9
10						10
11	30	Suta Tax Pay		135000		11
12		Cash			135000	12
13		Suta payment				13

Exercise 9-6A

$425,000 \times .2\% = 850$

1.

GENERAL JOURNAL
PAGE

	DATE	DESCRIPTION	POST. REF.	DEBIT	CREDIT	
1	Jan 1	WC Expense		85000		1
2		Cash			85000	2
3						3
4	Dec 31	Worker's Comp Exp.		1400		4
		Worker's Comp Pay			1400	
		To adj WC Ins.				

9-6B

2.

$396,000$
$-385,000$
$11,000$

$\$11,000 \times .2\% = \$22.00$

GENERAL JOURNAL
PAGE

	DATE	DESCRIPTION	POST. REF.	DEBIT	CREDIT	
1	2007 Dec 31	WC Expense		2200		1
2		Worker's Comp. Pay.			2200	2
3		To adj. WC Ins.				3
4						4

Problem 9-7A

		Taxable Earnings	
Name	**Total Earnings**	**Unemploy. Comp.**	**Social Security**
Barnum, Alex			
Duel, Richard			
Hunt, J. B.			
Larson, Susan			
Mercado, Denise			
Swan, Judy			
Yates, Keith			
Total			

2.

GENERAL JOURNAL   PAGE

	DATE	DESCRIPTION	POST. REF.	DEBIT	CREDIT	
1						1
2						2
3						3
4						4
5						5
6						6
7						7
8						8
9						9
10						10

Problem 9-8A

1.

GENERAL JOURNAL

PAGE

	DATE		DESCRIPTION	POST. REF.	DEBIT	CREDIT	
1							1
2							2
3							3
4							4
5							5
6							6
7							7
8							8
9							9
10							10
11							11
12							12
13							13
14							14
15							15
16							16
17							17
18							18
19							19
20							20
21							21
22							22
23							23
24							24
25							25
26							26
27							27
28							28
29							29
30							30
31							31
32							32
33							33
34							34

Problem 9-8A (Continued)

GENERAL JOURNAL   PAGE

	DATE	DESCRIPTION	POST. REF.	DEBIT	CREDIT	
1						1
2						2
3						3
4						4
5						5
6						6
7						7
8						8
9						9
10						10
11						11
12						12
13						13
14						14
15						15
16						16
17						17
18						18
19						19
20						20
21						21
22						22
23						23
24						24
25						25
26						26
27						27
28						28
29						29
30						30
31						31
32						32
33						33
34						34
35						35

Problem 9-8A (Concluded)

2.

Cash	101		Employ. Inc. Tax Pay.	211

Social Security Tax Payable	212		Medicare Tax Payable	213

Savings Bond Deductions Payable	218		FUTA Tax Payable	221

SUTA Tax Payable	222		Wages and Salaries Expense	511

Payroll Taxes Expense	530

Problem 9-9A

1.

_____

_____

_____

_____

_____

GENERAL JOURNAL   PAGE

	DATE		DESCRIPTION	POST. REF.	DEBIT	CREDIT	
1							1
2							2
3							3
4							4
5							5
6							6

2.

_____

_____

_____

_____

_____

GENERAL JOURNAL   PAGE

	DATE		DESCRIPTION	POST. REF.	DEBIT	CREDIT	
1							1
2							2
3							3
4							4
5							5
6							6

Problem 9-8B (Continued)

GENERAL JOURNAL

PAGE _____

	DATE		DESCRIPTION	POST. REF.	DEBIT	CREDIT	
1							1
2							2
3							3
4							4
5							5
6							6
7							7
8							8
9							9
10							10
11							11
12							12
13							13
14							14
15							15
16							16
17							17
18							18
19							19
20							20
21							21
22							22
23							23
24							24
25							25
26							26
27							27
28							28
29							29
30							30
31							31
32							32
33							33
34							34
35							35

Problem 9-8B (Concluded)

2.

Cash	101		Employ. Inc. Tax Pay.	211

Social Security Tax Payable	212		Medicare Tax Payable	213

Savings Bond Deductions Payable	218		FUTA Tax Payable	221

SUTA Tax Payable	222		Wages and Salaries Expense	511

Payroll Taxes Expense	530

Problem 9-9B

1.

_____
_____
_____
_____
_____
_____
_____

GENERAL JOURNAL   PAGE ____

	DATE		DESCRIPTION	POST. REF.	DEBIT	CREDIT	
1							1
2							2
3							3
4							4
5							5
6							6

2.

_____
_____
_____
_____
_____
_____
_____

GENERAL JOURNAL   PAGE ____

	DATE		DESCRIPTION	POST. REF.	DEBIT	CREDIT	
1							1
2							2
3							3
4							4
5							5
6							6

Problem 9-9B (Concluded)

3.

_____

_____

_____

_____

_____

GENERAL JOURNAL   PAGE _____

	DATE		DESCRIPTION	POST. REF.	DEBIT	CREDIT	
1							1
2							2
3							3
4							4

Mastery Problem

GENERAL JOURNAL

	DATE		DESCRIPTION	POST. REF.	DEBIT	CREDIT	
1							1
2							2
3							3
4							4
5							5
6							6
7							7
8							8
9							9
10							10
11							11
12							12
13							13
14							14
15							15
16							16
17							17
18							18
19							19
20							20
21							21
22							22
23							23
24							24
25							25
26							26
27							27
28							28
29							29
30							30
31							31
32							32
33							33
34							34
35							35

Mastery Problem (Concluded)

GENERAL JOURNAL

PAGE

	DATE		DESCRIPTION	POST. REF.	DEBIT	CREDIT	
1							1
2							2
3							3
4							4
5							5
6							6
7							7
8							8
9							9
10							10
11							11
12							12
13							13
14							14
15							15
16							16
17							17
18							18
19							19
20							20
21							21
22							22
23							23
24							24
25							25
26							26
27							27
28							28
29							29
30							30
31							31
32							32
33							33
34							34
35							35

Challenge Problem

1.

_____
_____
_____
_____
_____
_____

2.

GENERAL JOURNAL

PAGE ____

	DATE		DESCRIPTION	POST. REF.	DEBIT	CREDIT	
1							1
2							2
3							3
4							4
5							5
6							6
7							7

3.

_____
_____
_____
_____
_____

Exercise 10-1A

	Cash Basis	Modified Cash Basis	Accrual Basis
1. Purchase supplies on account.			
2. Make payment on asset previously purchased.			
3. Purchase supplies for cash.			
4. Purchase insurance for cash.			
5. Pay cash for wages.			
6. Pay cash for telephone expense.			
7. Pay cash for new equipment.			
8. Wages earned but not paid.			
9. Prepaid item purchased, partly used.			
10. Depreciation on long-term assets.			

Exercise 10-2A

COMBINATION JOURNAL

	DATE		CASH			DESCRIPTION	POST. REF.	
			DEBIT	CREDIT				
1								1
2								2
3								3
4								4
5								5
6								6
7								7
8								8
9								9
10								10
11								11
12								12
13								13
14								14
15								15
16								16
17								17
18								18
19								19
20								20
21								21
22								22
23								23
24								24
25								25
26								26
27								27
28								28
29								29
30								30
31								31
32								32
33								33
34								34

Exercise 10-2A (Concluded)

PAGE   1

	GENERAL						
	DEBIT	CREDIT					
1							1
2							2
3							3
4							4
5							5
6							6
7							7
8							8
9							9
10							10
11							11
12							12
13							13
14							14
15							15
16							16
17							17
18							18
19							19
20							20
21							21
22							22
23							23
24							24
25							25
26							26
27							27
28							28
29							29
30							30
31							31
32							32
33							33
34							34

Exercise 10-3A

COMBINATION JOURNAL

| DATE | CASH | | DESCRIPTION | POST. REF. |
	DEBIT	CREDIT		
1				1
2				2
3				3
4				4
5				5
6				6
7				7
8				8
9				9
10				10
11				11
12				12
13				13
14				14
15				15
16				16
17				17
18				18
19				19
20				20
21				21
22				22
23				23
24				24
25				25
26				26
27				27
28				28

Proving the Combination Journal:

Exercise 10-3A (Concluded)

PAGE 1

	GENERAL				REPAIR FEES CREDIT			WAGES EXPENSE DEBIT		
	DEBIT		CREDIT							
1											1
2											2
3											3
4											4
5											5
6											6
7											7
8											8
9											9
10											10
11											11
12											12
13											13
14											14
15											15
16											16
17											17
18											18
19											19
20											20
21											21
22											22
23											23
24											24
25											25
26											26
27											27
28											28

Problem 10-4A

1. and 4.

COMBINATION JOURNAL

	DATE		CASH				DESCRIPTION	POST. REF.	
			DEBIT		CREDIT				
1									1
2									2
3									3
4									4
5									5
6									6
7									7
8									8
9									9
10									10
11									11
12									12
13									13
14									14
15									15
16									16
17									17
18									18
19									19
20									20
21									21
22									22
23									23
24									24
25									25
26									26
27									27
28									28
29									29
30									30
31									31
32									32
33									33
34									34

Problem 10-4A (Continued)

PAGE 1

	GENERAL						
	DEBIT	CREDIT					
1							
2							
3							
4							
5							
6							
7							
8							
9							
10							
11							
12							
13							
14							
15							
16							
17							
18							
19							
20							
21							
22							
23							
24							
25							
26							
27							
28							
29							
30							
31							
32							
33							
34							

Problem 10-4A (Continued)

2. **Cash Balance, January 12:**

_____

_____

_____

_____

3. **Proving the Combination Journal:**

_____

_____

_____

_____

_____

_____

_____

5.

_____

_____

_____

ACCOUNT	ACCT. NO.	DEBIT BALANCE	CREDIT BALANCE

Problem 10-4A (Continued)

4.

PARTIAL GENERAL LEDGER

ACCOUNT Cash   ACCOUNT NO. 101

DATE	ITEM	POST. REF.	DEBIT	CREDIT	BALANCE DEBIT	BALANCE CREDIT

ACCOUNT Office Supplies   ACCOUNT NO. 142

DATE	ITEM	POST. REF.	DEBIT	CREDIT	BALANCE DEBIT	BALANCE CREDIT

ACCOUNT Office Equipment   ACCOUNT NO. 181

DATE	ITEM	POST. REF.	DEBIT	CREDIT	BALANCE DEBIT	BALANCE CREDIT

ACCOUNT Accounts Payable   ACCOUNT NO. 202

DATE	ITEM	POST. REF.	DEBIT	CREDIT	BALANCE DEBIT	BALANCE CREDIT

Problem 10-4A (Continued)

ACCOUNT Angela McWharton, Capital   ACCOUNT NO. 311

DATE	ITEM	POST. REF.	DEBIT	CREDIT	BALANCE DEBIT	BALANCE CREDIT

ACCOUNT Angela McWharton, Drawing   ACCOUNT NO. 312

DATE	ITEM	POST. REF.	DEBIT	CREDIT	BALANCE DEBIT	BALANCE CREDIT

ACCOUNT Nursing Care Fees   ACCOUNT NO. 401

DATE	ITEM	POST. REF.	DEBIT	CREDIT	BALANCE DEBIT	BALANCE CREDIT

ACCOUNT Wages Expense   ACCOUNT NO. 511

DATE	ITEM	POST. REF.	DEBIT	CREDIT	BALANCE DEBIT	BALANCE CREDIT

ACCOUNT Advertising Expense   ACCOUNT NO. 512

DATE	ITEM	POST. REF.	DEBIT	CREDIT	BALANCE DEBIT	BALANCE CREDIT

Problem 10-4A (Concluded)

ACCOUNT   Rent Expense   ACCOUNT NO.   521

DATE	ITEM	POST. REF.	DEBIT	CREDIT	BALANCE	
					DEBIT	CREDIT

ACCOUNT   Telephone Expense   ACCOUNT NO.   525

DATE	ITEM	POST. REF.	DEBIT	CREDIT	BALANCE	
					DEBIT	CREDIT

ACCOUNT   Transportation Expense   ACCOUNT NO.   526

DATE	ITEM	POST. REF.	DEBIT	CREDIT	BALANCE	
					DEBIT	CREDIT

ACCOUNT   Electricity Expense   ACCOUNT NO.   533

DATE	ITEM	POST. REF.	DEBIT	CREDIT	BALANCE	
					DEBIT	CREDIT

ACCOUNT   Miscellaneous Expense   ACCOUNT NO.   549

DATE	ITEM	POST. REF.	DEBIT	CREDIT	BALANCE	
					DEBIT	CREDIT

Problem 10-5A

1. and 4.

COMBINATION JOURNAL

	DATE		CASH			DESCRIPTION	POST. REF.	
			DEBIT	CREDIT				
1								1
2								2
3								3
4								4
5								5
6								6
7								7
8								8
9								9
10								10
11								11
12								12
13								13
14								14
15								15
16								16
17								17
18								18
19								19
20								20
21								21
22								22
23								23
24								24
25								25
26								26
27								27
28								28
29								29
30								30
31								31
32								32
33								33
34								34

Problem 10-5A (Continued)

PAGE 5

	GENERAL			TAILORING FEES CREDIT	WAGES EXPENSE DEBIT	ADVERTISING EXPENSE DEBIT	
	DEBIT		CREDIT				
1							1
2							2
3							3
4							4
5							5
6							6
7							7
8							8
9							9
10							10
11							11
12							12
13							13
14							14
15							15
16							16
17							17
18							18
19							19
20							20
21							21
22							22
23							23
24							24
25							25
26							26
27							27
28							28
29							29
30							30
31							31
32							32
33							33
34							34

Problem 10-5A (Continued)

2. Cash Balance, November 12:

_____

_____

_____

_____

_____

_____

_____

3. Proving the Combination Journal:

_____

_____

_____

_____

_____

_____

_____

_____

_____

_____

4.

GENERAL LEDGER

ACCOUNT   Cash   ACCOUNT NO.   101

DATE	ITEM	POST. REF.	DEBIT	CREDIT	BALANCE DEBIT	BALANCE CREDIT

ACCOUNT   Tailoring Supplies   ACCOUNT NO.   141

DATE	ITEM	POST. REF.	DEBIT	CREDIT	BALANCE DEBIT	BALANCE CREDIT

Problem 10-5A (Continued)

ACCOUNT   Office Supplies   ACCOUNT NO.   142

DATE	ITEM	POST. REF.	DEBIT	CREDIT	BALANCE	
					DEBIT	CREDIT

ACCOUNT   Prepaid Insurance   ACCOUNT NO.   145

DATE	ITEM	POST. REF.	DEBIT	CREDIT	BALANCE	
					DEBIT	CREDIT

ACCOUNT   Tailoring Equipment   ACCOUNT NO.   188

DATE	ITEM	POST. REF.	DEBIT	CREDIT	BALANCE	
					DEBIT	CREDIT

ACCOUNT   Accumulated Depreciation—Tailoring Equipment   ACCOUNT NO.   188.1

DATE	ITEM	POST. REF.	DEBIT	CREDIT	BALANCE	
					DEBIT	CREDIT

Problem 10-5A (Continued)

ACCOUNT Accounts Payable   ACCOUNT NO. 202

DATE	ITEM	POST. REF.	DEBIT	CREDIT	BALANCE	
					DEBIT	CREDIT

ACCOUNT Sue Reyton, Capital   ACCOUNT NO. 311

DATE	ITEM	POST. REF.	DEBIT	CREDIT	BALANCE	
					DEBIT	CREDIT

ACCOUNT Sue Reyton, Drawing   ACCOUNT NO. 312

DATE	ITEM	POST. REF.	DEBIT	CREDIT	BALANCE	
					DEBIT	CREDIT

ACCOUNT Income Summary   ACCOUNT NO. 313

DATE	ITEM	POST. REF.	DEBIT	CREDIT	BALANCE	
					DEBIT	CREDIT

Problem 10-5A (Continued)

ACCOUNT Tailoring Fees   ACCOUNT NO. 401

DATE	ITEM	POST. REF.	DEBIT	CREDIT	BALANCE DEBIT	BALANCE CREDIT

ACCOUNT Wages Expense   ACCOUNT NO. 511

DATE	ITEM	POST. REF.	DEBIT	CREDIT	BALANCE DEBIT	BALANCE CREDIT

ACCOUNT Advertising Expense   ACCOUNT NO. 512

DATE	ITEM	POST. REF.	DEBIT	CREDIT	BALANCE DEBIT	BALANCE CREDIT

ACCOUNT Rent Expense   ACCOUNT NO. 521

DATE	ITEM	POST. REF.	DEBIT	CREDIT	BALANCE DEBIT	BALANCE CREDIT

Problem 10-5A (Continued)

ACCOUNT   Office Supplies Expense   ACCOUNT NO.   523

DATE	ITEM	POST. REF.	DEBIT	CREDIT	BALANCE DEBIT	BALANCE CREDIT

ACCOUNT   Tailoring Supplies Expense   ACCOUNT NO.   524

DATE	ITEM	POST. REF.	DEBIT	CREDIT	BALANCE DEBIT	BALANCE CREDIT

ACCOUNT   Telephone Expense   ACCOUNT NO.   525

DATE	ITEM	POST. REF.	DEBIT	CREDIT	BALANCE DEBIT	BALANCE CREDIT

ACCOUNT   Electricity Expense   ACCOUNT NO.   533

DATE	ITEM	POST. REF.	DEBIT	CREDIT	BALANCE DEBIT	BALANCE CREDIT

Problem 10-5A (Continued)

ACCOUNT Insurance Expense   ACCOUNT NO.   535

DATE	ITEM	POST. REF.	DEBIT	CREDIT	BALANCE	
					DEBIT	CREDIT

ACCOUNT Depreciation Expense—Tailoring Equipment   ACCOUNT NO.   542

DATE	ITEM	POST. REF.	DEBIT	CREDIT	BALANCE	
					DEBIT	CREDIT

ACCOUNT Miscellaneous Expense   ACCOUNT NO.   549

DATE	ITEM	POST. REF.	DEBIT	CREDIT	BALANCE	
					DEBIT	CREDIT

Problem 10-5A (Continued)

5.

	TRIAL BALANCE		ADJUSTMENTS	
	DEBIT	CREDIT	DEBIT	CREDIT
1				
2				
3				
4				
5				
6				
7				
8				
9				
10				
11				
12				
13				
14				
15				
16				
17				
18				
19				
20				
21				
22				
23				
24				
25				
26				
27				
28				
29				
30				
31				
32				

Problem 10-5A (Continued)

ADJUSTED TRIAL BALANCE		INCOME STATEMENT		BALANCE SHEET	
DEBIT	CREDIT	DEBIT	CREDIT	DEBIT	CREDIT

Problem 10-5A (Continued)

6.

Problem 10-5A (Continued)

Problem 10-5A (Continued)

7.

COMBINATION JOURNAL

	DATE	CASH			DESCRIPTION	POST. REF.	
		DEBIT		CREDIT			
1							1
2							2
3							3
4							4
5							5
6							6
7							7
8							8
9							9
10							10
11							11
12							12
13							13
14							14
15							15
16							16
17							17
18							18
19							19
20							20
21							21
22							22
23							23
24							24
25							25
26							26
27							27
28							28
29							29
30							30
31							31
32							32
33							33
34							34

Problem 10-5A (Concluded)

GENERAL		TAILORING FEES CREDIT	WAGES EXPENSE DEBIT	ADVERTISING EXPENSE DEBIT	
DEBIT	CREDIT				
					1
					2
					3
					4
					5
					6
					7
					8
					9
					10
					11
					12
					13
					14
					15
					16
					17
					18
					19
					20
					21
					22
					23
					24
					25
					26
					27
					28
					29
					30
					31
					32
					33
					34

Exercise 10-1B

	Cash Basis	Modified Cash Basis	Accrual Basis

1. Office Equipment
     Cash
          Purchased equipment for cash			

2. Office Equipment
     Accounts Payable
          Purchased equipment on account			

3. Cash
     Revenue
          Cash receipts for week			

4. Accounts Receivable
     Revenue
          Services performed on account			

5. Prepaid Insurance
     Cash
          Purchased prepaid asset			

6. Supplies
     Accounts Payable
          Purchased prepaid asset			

7. Telephone Expense
     Cash
          Paid telephone bill			

8. Wages Expense
     Cash
          Paid wages for month			

9. Accounts Payable
     Cash
          Made payment on account			

10. Supplies Expense Supplies			

	Cash Basis	Modified Cash Basis	Accrual Basis
11. Wages Expense Wages Payable			
12. Depreciation Expense—Office Equipment Accum. Depr. —Office Equipment			

Exercise 10-2B

COMBINATION JOURNAL

	DATE		CASH			DESCRIPTION	POST. REF.	
			DEBIT		CREDIT			
1								1
2								2
3								3
4								4
5								5
6								6
7								7
8								8
9								9
10								10
11								11
12								12
13								13
14								14
15								15
16								16
17								17
18								18
19								19
20								20
21								21
22								22
23								23
24								24
25								25
26								26
27								27
28								28
29								29
30								30
31								31
32								32
33								33
34								34

Name _____

Exercise 10-2B (Concluded)

PAGE 1

	GENERAL				
	DEBIT	CREDIT			
1					
2					
3					
4					
5					
6					
7					
8					
9					
10					
11					
12					
13					
14					
15					
16					
17					
18					
19					
20					
21					
22					
23					
24					
25					
26					
27					
28					
29					
30					
31					
32					
33					
34					

Exercise 10-3B

COMBINATION JOURNAL

| DATE | CASH | | DESCRIPTION | POST. REF. |
	DEBIT	CREDIT		
1				1
2				2
3				3
4				4
5				5
6				6
7				7
8				8
9				9
10				10
11				11
12				12
13				13
14				14
15				15
16				16
17				17
18				18
19				19
20				20
21				21
22				22
23				23
24				24
25				25
26				26
27				27
28				28

Proving the Combination Journal:

Exercise 10-3B (Concluded)

PAGE 1

	GENERAL			DELIVERY FEES CREDIT	WAGES EXPENSE DEBIT	
	DEBIT		CREDIT			
1						1
2						2
3						3
4						4
5						5
6						6
7						7
8						8
9						9
10						10
11						11
12						12
13						13
14						14
15						15
16						16
17						17
18						18
19						19
20						20
21						21
22						22
23						23
24						24
25						25
26						26
27						27
28						28

Problem 10-4B

1. and 4.

COMBINATION JOURNAL

DATE	CASH DEBIT	CASH CREDIT	DESCRIPTION	POST. REF.
1				1
2				2
3				3
4				4
5				5
6				6
7				7
8				8
9				9
10				10
11				11
12				12
13				13
14				14
15				15
16				16
17				17
18				18
19				19
20				20
21				21
22				22
23				23
24				24
25				25
26				26
27				27
28				28
29				29
30				30
31				31
32				32
33				33
34				34

Problem 10-4B (Continued)

PAGE 1

	GENERAL							
	DEBIT	CREDIT						
1								
2								
3								
4								
5								
6								
7								
8								
9								
10								
11								
12								
13								
14								
15								
16								
17								
18								
19								
20								
21								
22								
23								
24								
25								
26								
27								
28								
29								
30								
31								
32								
33								
34								

Problem 10-4B (Continued)

2. **Cash Balance, July 14:**

_____

_____

_____

_____

3. **Proving the Combination Journal:**

_____

_____

_____

_____

_____

_____

_____

5.

_____

_____

_____

ACCOUNT	ACCT. NO.	DEBIT BALANCE	CREDIT BALANCE	

Problem 10-4B (Continued)

4.

GENERAL LEDGER

ACCOUNT   Cash   ACCOUNT NO.   101

DATE		ITEM	POST. REF.	DEBIT	CREDIT	BALANCE	
						DEBIT	CREDIT

ACCOUNT   Office Supplies   ACCOUNT NO.   142

DATE		ITEM	POST. REF.	DEBIT	CREDIT	BALANCE	
						DEBIT	CREDIT

ACCOUNT   Skiing Equipment   ACCOUNT NO.   183

DATE		ITEM	POST. REF.	DEBIT	CREDIT	BALANCE	
						DEBIT	CREDIT

ACCOUNT   Accounts Payable   ACCOUNT NO.   202

DATE		ITEM	POST. REF.	DEBIT	CREDIT	BALANCE	
						DEBIT	CREDIT

Problem 10-4B (Continued)

ACCOUNT J. B. Hoyt, Capital   ACCOUNT NO. 311

DATE	ITEM	POST. REF.	DEBIT	CREDIT	BALANCE DEBIT	BALANCE CREDIT

ACCOUNT J. B. Hoyt, Drawing   ACCOUNT NO. 312

DATE	ITEM	POST. REF.	DEBIT	CREDIT	BALANCE DEBIT	BALANCE CREDIT

ACCOUNT Training Fees   ACCOUNT NO. 401

DATE	ITEM	POST. REF.	DEBIT	CREDIT	BALANCE DEBIT	BALANCE CREDIT

ACCOUNT Wages Expense   ACCOUNT NO. 511

DATE	ITEM	POST. REF.	DEBIT	CREDIT	BALANCE DEBIT	BALANCE CREDIT

ACCOUNT Rent Expense   ACCOUNT NO. 521

DATE	ITEM	POST. REF.	DEBIT	CREDIT	BALANCE DEBIT	BALANCE CREDIT

Problem 10-4B (Concluded)

ACCOUNT Telephone Expense   ACCOUNT NO. 525

DATE	ITEM	POST. REF.	DEBIT	CREDIT	BALANCE	
					DEBIT	CREDIT

ACCOUNT Transportation Expense   ACCOUNT NO. 526

DATE	ITEM	POST. REF.	DEBIT	CREDIT	BALANCE	
					DEBIT	CREDIT

ACCOUNT Electricity Expense   ACCOUNT NO. 533

DATE	ITEM	POST. REF.	DEBIT	CREDIT	BALANCE	
					DEBIT	CREDIT

ACCOUNT Repair Expense   ACCOUNT NO. 537

DATE	ITEM	POST. REF.	DEBIT	CREDIT	BALANCE	
					DEBIT	CREDIT

ACCOUNT Miscellaneous Expense   ACCOUNT NO. 549

DATE	ITEM	POST. REF.	DEBIT	CREDIT	BALANCE	
					DEBIT	CREDIT

Problem 10-5B

1. and 4.

COMBINATION JOURNAL

	DATE		CASH			DESCRIPTION	POST. REF.	
			DEBIT	CREDIT				
1								1
2								2
3								3
4								4
5								5
6								6
7								7
8								8
9								9
10								10
11								11
12								12
13								13
14								14
15								15
16								16
17								17
18								18
19								19
20								20
21								21
22								22
23								23
24								24
25								25
26								26
27								27
28								28
29								29
30								30
31								31
32								32
33								33
34								34

Problem 10-5B (Continued)

PAGE 5

	GENERAL			LAWN CARE	REPAIR EXPENSE	WAGES EXPENSE	
	DEBIT		CREDIT	FEES CREDIT	DEBIT	DEBIT	
1							1
2							2
3							3
4							4
5							5
6							6
7							7
8							8
9							9
10							10
11							11
12							12
13							13
14							14
15							15
16							16
17							17
18							18
19							19
20							20
21							21
22							22
23							23
24							24
25							25
26							26
27							27
28							28
29							29
30							30
31							31
32							32
33							33
34							34

Problem 10-5B (Continued)

2. Cash Balance, June 12:

_____
_____
_____
_____
_____
_____
_____

3. Proving the Combination Journal:

_____
_____
_____
_____
_____
_____
_____
_____

4.

GENERAL LEDGER

ACCOUNT Cash   ACCOUNT NO. 101

DATE	ITEM	POST. REF.	DEBIT	CREDIT	BALANCE	
					DEBIT	CREDIT

ACCOUNT Lawn Care Supplies   ACCOUNT NO. 141

DATE	ITEM	POST. REF.	DEBIT	CREDIT	BALANCE	
					DEBIT	CREDIT

Problem 10-5B (Continued)

ACCOUNT   Office Supplies   ACCOUNT NO.   142

DATE	ITEM	POST. REF.	DEBIT	CREDIT	BALANCE	
					DEBIT	CREDIT

ACCOUNT   Prepaid Insurance   ACCOUNT NO.   145

DATE	ITEM	POST. REF.	DEBIT	CREDIT	BALANCE	
					DEBIT	CREDIT

ACCOUNT   Lawn Care Equipment   ACCOUNT NO.   189

DATE	ITEM	POST. REF.	DEBIT	CREDIT	BALANCE	
					DEBIT	CREDIT

ACCOUNT   Accumulated Depreciation—Lawn Care Equipment   ACCOUNT NO.   189.1

DATE	ITEM	POST. REF.	DEBIT	CREDIT	BALANCE	
					DEBIT	CREDIT

Problem 10-5B (Continued)

ACCOUNT **Accounts Payable**   ACCOUNT NO. **202**

DATE	ITEM	POST. REF.	DEBIT	CREDIT	BALANCE DEBIT	BALANCE CREDIT

ACCOUNT **Molly Claussen, Capital**   ACCOUNT NO. **311**

DATE	ITEM	POST. REF.	DEBIT	CREDIT	BALANCE DEBIT	BALANCE CREDIT

ACCOUNT **Molly Claussen, Drawing**   ACCOUNT NO. **312**

DATE	ITEM	POST. REF.	DEBIT	CREDIT	BALANCE DEBIT	BALANCE CREDIT

ACCOUNT **Income Summary**   ACCOUNT NO. **313**

DATE	ITEM	POST. REF.	DEBIT	CREDIT	BALANCE DEBIT	BALANCE CREDIT

Problem 10-5B (Continued)

ACCOUNT   Lawn Care Fees   ACCOUNT NO.   401

DATE	ITEM	POST. REF.	DEBIT	CREDIT	BALANCE	
					DEBIT	CREDIT

ACCOUNT   Wages Expense   ACCOUNT NO.   511

DATE	ITEM	POST. REF.	DEBIT	CREDIT	BALANCE	
					DEBIT	CREDIT

ACCOUNT   Rent Expense   ACCOUNT NO.   521

DATE	ITEM	POST. REF.	DEBIT	CREDIT	BALANCE	
					DEBIT	CREDIT

ACCOUNT   Office Supplies Expense   ACCOUNT NO.   523

DATE	ITEM	POST. REF.	DEBIT	CREDIT	BALANCE	
					DEBIT	CREDIT

Problem 10-5B (Continued)

ACCOUNT Lawn Care Supplies Expense   ACCOUNT NO. 524

DATE	ITEM	POST. REF.	DEBIT	CREDIT	BALANCE	
					DEBIT	CREDIT

ACCOUNT Telephone Expense   ACCOUNT NO. 525

DATE	ITEM	POST. REF.	DEBIT	CREDIT	BALANCE	
					DEBIT	CREDIT

ACCOUNT Electricity Expense   ACCOUNT NO. 533

DATE	ITEM	POST. REF.	DEBIT	CREDIT	BALANCE	
					DEBIT	CREDIT

ACCOUNT Insurance Expense   ACCOUNT NO. 535

DATE	ITEM	POST. REF.	DEBIT	CREDIT	BALANCE	
					DEBIT	CREDIT

Problem 10-5B (Continued)

ACCOUNT   Repair Expense   ACCOUNT NO.   537

DATE		ITEM	POST. REF.	DEBIT	CREDIT	BALANCE	
						DEBIT	CREDIT

ACCOUNT   Gas and Oil Expense   ACCOUNT NO.   538

DATE		ITEM	POST. REF.	DEBIT	CREDIT	BALANCE	
						DEBIT	CREDIT

ACCOUNT   Depreciation Expense—Lawn Care Equipment   ACCOUNT NO.   542

DATE		ITEM	POST. REF.	DEBIT	CREDIT	BALANCE	
						DEBIT	CREDIT

Problem 10-5B (Continued)

5.

	TRIAL BALANCE		ADJUSTMENTS	
	DEBIT	CREDIT	DEBIT	CREDIT
1				
2				
3				
4				
5				
6				
7				
8				
9				
10				
11				
12				
13				
14				
15				
16				
17				
18				
19				
20				
21				
22				
23				
24				
25				
26				
27				
28				
29				
30				
31				
32				

Problem 10-5B (Continued)

ADJUSTED TRIAL BALANCE		INCOME STATEMENT		BALANCE SHEET		
DEBIT	CREDIT	DEBIT	CREDIT	DEBIT	CREDIT	
						1
						2
						3
						4
						5
						6
						7
						8
						9
						10
						11
						12
						13
						14
						15
						16
						17
						18
						19
						20
						21
						22
						23
						24
						25
						26
						27
						28
						29
						30
						31
						32

Problem 10-5B (Continued)

6.

Problem 10-5B (Continued)

Problem 10-5B (Continued)

7.

COMBINATION JOURNAL

	DATE		CASH				DESCRIPTION	POST. REF.	
			DEBIT		CREDIT				
1									1
2									2
3									3
4									4
5									5
6									6
7									7
8									8
9									9
10									10
11									11
12									12
13									13
14									14
15									15
16									16
17									17
18									18
19									19
20									20
21									21
22									22
23									23
24									24
25									25
26									26
27									27
28									28
29									29
30									30
31									31
32									32
33									33
34									34

Problem 10-5B (Concluded)

PAGE   6

	GENERAL		LAWN CARE FEES CREDIT	REPAIR EXPENSE DEBIT	WAGES EXPENSE DEBIT	
	DEBIT	CREDIT				
1						1
2						2
3						3
4						4
5						5
6						6
7						7
8						8
9						9
10						10
11						11
12						12
13						13
14						14
15						15
16						16
17						17
18						18
19						19
20						20
21						21
22						22
23						23
24						24
25						25
26						26
27						27
28						28
29						29
30						30
31						31
32						32
33						33
34						34

Mastery Problem

1. **The Combination Journal can be found on pages WP-356 and WP-357**

2. **Proving the Combination Journal:**

_____

_____

_____

_____

_____

_____

_____

3.

GENERAL LEDGER

ACCOUNT Cash   ACCOUNT NO. 101

DATE	ITEM	POST. REF.	DEBIT	CREDIT	BALANCE	
					DEBIT	CREDIT

ACCOUNT Office Supplies   ACCOUNT NO. 142

DATE	ITEM	POST. REF.	DEBIT	CREDIT	BALANCE	
					DEBIT	CREDIT

Mastery Problem (Continued)

ACCOUNT   Food Supplies   ACCOUNT NO.   144

DATE	ITEM	POST. REF.	DEBIT	CREDIT	BALANCE	
					DEBIT	CREDIT

ACCOUNT   Tennis Facilities   ACCOUNT NO.   184

DATE	ITEM	POST. REF.	DEBIT	CREDIT	BALANCE	
					DEBIT	CREDIT

ACCOUNT   Accumulated Depreciation—Tennis Facilities   ACCOUNT NO.   184.1

DATE	ITEM	POST. REF.	DEBIT	CREDIT	BALANCE	
					DEBIT	CREDIT

ACCOUNT   Exercise Equipment   ACCOUNT NO.   186

DATE	ITEM	POST. REF.	DEBIT	CREDIT	BALANCE	
					DEBIT	CREDIT

Mastery Problem (Continued)

ACCOUNT   Accumulated Depreciation—Exercise Equipment   ACCOUNT NO.   186.1

DATE	ITEM	POST. REF.	DEBIT	CREDIT	BALANCE	
					DEBIT	CREDIT

ACCOUNT   Accounts Payable   ACCOUNT NO.   202

DATE	ITEM	POST. REF.	DEBIT	CREDIT	BALANCE	
					DEBIT	CREDIT

ACCOUNT   John McRoe, Capital   ACCOUNT NO.   311

DATE	ITEM	POST. REF.	DEBIT	CREDIT	BALANCE	
					DEBIT	CREDIT

ACCOUNT   John McRoe, Drawing   ACCOUNT NO.   312

DATE	ITEM	POST. REF.	DEBIT	CREDIT	BALANCE	
					DEBIT	CREDIT

Mastery Problem (Continued)

ACCOUNT   Income Summary   ACCOUNT NO.   313

DATE	ITEM	POST. REF.	DEBIT	CREDIT	BALANCE	
					DEBIT	CREDIT

ACCOUNT   Registration Fees   ACCOUNT NO.   401

DATE	ITEM	POST. REF.	DEBIT	CREDIT	BALANCE	
					DEBIT	CREDIT

ACCOUNT   Wages Expense   ACCOUNT NO.   511

DATE	ITEM	POST. REF.	DEBIT	CREDIT	BALANCE	
					DEBIT	CREDIT

ACCOUNT   Rent Expense   ACCOUNT NO.   521

DATE	ITEM	POST. REF.	DEBIT	CREDIT	BALANCE	
					DEBIT	CREDIT

ACCOUNT   Office Supplies Expense   ACCOUNT NO.   523

DATE	ITEM	POST. REF.	DEBIT	CREDIT	BALANCE	
					DEBIT	CREDIT

Mastery Problem (Continued)

ACCOUNT   Food Supplies Expense   ACCOUNT NO.   524

DATE	ITEM	POST. REF.	DEBIT	CREDIT	BALANCE	
					DEBIT	CREDIT

ACCOUNT   Telephone Expense   ACCOUNT NO.   525

DATE	ITEM	POST. REF.	DEBIT	CREDIT	BALANCE	
					DEBIT	CREDIT

ACCOUNT   Utilities Expense   ACCOUNT NO.   533

DATE	ITEM	POST. REF.	DEBIT	CREDIT	BALANCE	
					DEBIT	CREDIT

ACCOUNT   Insurance Expense   ACCOUNT NO.   535

DATE	ITEM	POST. REF.	DEBIT	CREDIT	BALANCE	
					DEBIT	CREDIT

ACCOUNT   Postage Expense   ACCOUNT NO.   536

DATE	ITEM	POST. REF.	DEBIT	CREDIT	BALANCE	
					DEBIT	CREDIT

Mastery Problem (Continued)

ACCOUNT   Depreciation Expense—Tennis Facilities   ACCOUNT NO.   541

DATE	ITEM	POST. REF.	DEBIT	CREDIT	BALANCE	
					DEBIT	CREDIT

ACCOUNT   Depreciation Expense—Exercise Equipment   ACCOUNT NO.   542

DATE	ITEM	POST. REF.	DEBIT	CREDIT	BALANCE	
					DEBIT	CREDIT

Mastery Problem

1.

COMBINATION JOURNAL

	DATE		CASH		DESCRIPTION	POST. REF.	
			DEBIT	CREDIT			
1							1
2							2
3							3
4							4
5							5
6							6
7							7
8							8
9							9
10							10
11							11
12							12
13							13
14							14
15							15
16							16
17							17
18							18
19							19
20							20
21							21
22							22
23							23
24							24
25							25
26							26
27							27
28							28
29							29
30							30
31							31
32							32
33							33
34							34

Mastery Problem (Continued)

	GENERAL		REGISTRATION FEES CREDIT	WAGES EXPENSE DEBIT	FOOD SUPPLIES DEBIT	
	DEBIT	CREDIT				
1						1
2						2
3						3
4						4
5						5
6						6
7						7
8						8
9						9
10						10
11						11
12						12
13						13
14						14
15						15
16						16
17						17
18						18
19						19
20						20
21						21
22						22
23						23
24						24
25						25
26						26
27						27
28						28
29						29
30						30
31						31
32						32
33						33
34						34

Mastery Problem (Concluded)

4.

ACCOUNT	ACCT. NO.	DEBIT BALANCE	CREDIT BALANCE

Challenge Problem

Resler Financial Consulting
Income Statements
For Month Ended June 20--

	Cash Basis		Modified Cash Basis		Accrual Basis	

Notes

End Page of Working Papers